B2B SALES FOR THE ENTREPRENEUR

A Step-by-Step Sales Guide for First-Time Founders

B2B SALES FOR THE ENTREPRENEUR

A Step-by-Step Sales Guide for First-Time Founders

"Sales struggles to a scalable success"

GARRY MANSELL

BROWN
DOG
BOOKS

Published under licence by Brown Dog Books and

The Self-Publishing Partnership Ltd,
10b Greenway Farm, Bath Rd, Wick, nr. Bath BS30 5RL, UK

www.selfpublishingpartnership.co.uk

ISBN printed book: 978-1-83952-958-0
ISBN e-book: 978-1-83952-959-7

Cover design by Kevin Rylands
Internal design by Jenny Watson Design

Printed and bound in the UK
This book is printed on FSC® certified paper

MIX
Paper | Supporting
responsible forestry
FSC® C013604
FSC
www.fsc.org

This book is dedicated to

Will Mayes and his Executive Team at Layrd Design Ltd: Eleanor Penny, Emily Batten, Gina Clarke and Emily Gray. They encouraged me to use a course on 'Selling as a Founder' which I had developed and been presenting for eighteen months, having already delivered it to them, and to transform it into this book.

Thank you all for being the catalyst and for encouraging me to do what I had vowed I would never do again: write another book!

CONTENTS

INTRODUCTION

The product is perfect. Your B2B innovation, the one in which you've invested months, perhaps years, of your life, is finally ready. There's just one issue. The order book is stubbornly blank. That meticulously researched list of 'ideal customers' on your screen suddenly feels less like a goldmine and more like a catalogue of impending, awkward conversations you're utterly terrified to initiate.

A knot tightens in your stomach. It's not sufficient to build it. Someone actually has to sell this thing.

And then, the even more chilling realisation: that someone is you, isn't it? And you feel you haven't the faintest idea where to start.

If that sounds even remotely familiar, you're in the right place.

Welcome to 'B2B Sales for the Entrepreneur: A step-by-step sales guide for First-Time Founders'. If you're here, chances are you're a driven entrepreneur with a new venture on your hands, ready to take your innovative product or service to market. The road ahead is exciting yet littered with challenges, particularly in sales.

This book is crafted specifically for you – the passionate founder who may have little to no sales experience but possesses a burning desire to succeed.

In the dynamic world of startups, as a founder, you wear many hats. Wearing the salesperson's hat is an inevitable part of your journey. Selling your product or service, especially when you are new to the market, involves a learning curve to which you must quickly adapt. It presents an opportunity to harness your belief in your product and channel your enthusiasm directly to potential customers. This

book aims to guide you through the process, focusing less on sales theory and more on practical strategies you can implement today.

We explore the lean sales approach, which aligns with the lean startup methodology, where experimentation and iteration are essential. You'll learn how to effectively navigate the sales landscape without a large budget or a sales team. From identifying your first ideal customers to crafting a compelling value proposition, this book provides clear, actionable steps to generate leads and close deals, all while capitalising on your unique position as a founder.

Furthermore, this book acknowledges the emotional journey you will undertake. The highs of securing new clients and the lows of rejection are part of the entrepreneurial rollercoaster. Developing resilience, empathy and maintaining the right mindset are as crucial as any sales technique you will learn. By preparing you for these emotional challenges, this guide will assist you in building the confidence to confront the unknown.

As you move through these pages, remember that every great business was once at the stage you find yourself in today. Embrace the journey, learn from every interaction and shape the future of sales for your business.

Whether you are closing your first deal or preparing to hire your first salesperson, the skills you acquire here will serve as the backbone of your growing enterprise.

WHO IS THIS BOOK FOR?

This book is written for first-time founders who are building something they believe in – and now face the reality that someone needs to sell it.

You might be an engineer, a product manager, a consultant, or a creative – someone who never thought they'd need to 'do sales'. But here you are, at the sharp end, talking to prospective customers, pitching your product, handling objections and trying to figure out what works.

You may have never sold anything professionally. You may not even feel like a 'salesperson'. That's perfectly fine. You don't need to become someone else – you need to become more of who you already are, but with structure, confidence and a toolkit that works for you.

This book is for founders who:

- Are launching their first B2B startup or early-stage business
- Need to bring in their first paying customers – without a sales team
- Want to sell without feeling pushy or inauthentic
- Are looking to build repeatable sales habits alongside their product
- Are learning to balance passion with process, rejection with resilience

If you've ever stared at a blank CRM, dreaded a cold email, flinched at the word 'follow-up', or wondered how others manage to close deals with ease – this book is for you. It's practical, honest and shaped by the real conversations and challenges that early-stage entrepreneurs face every day.

You won't find jargon, scripts, or silver bullets here. Instead, you'll find a step-by-step guide to developing your mindset, sharpening your message, finding the right customers and turning those early wins into sustainable growth.

Sales might not be the job you asked for – but it could be the most important one you do.

PART 1

THE INNER GAME OF SELLING

Before you learn how to sell, you must believe that you can. This section of the book helps you establish the mental foundation necessary for successful, sustainable founder-led sales. You'll change your perspective on selling, reframe your fear of rejection and begin to view sales not as a chore – but as an entrepreneurial superpower.

Chapter Zero

SALES MYTHS TO UNLEARN

'You can't build a reputation on what you are going to do.'
– Henry Ford

I f you're reading this, it's likely that you've already undergone one of the most significant mindset shifts of your career: you've recognised that selling is now part of your job. Not later. Now. And that's no insignificant matter.

But before you start learning how to sell, you need to make some space. Most first-time founders enter sales carrying a heavy burden of assumptions – half-truths, myths and second-hand stories about what sales is and what it isn't. These can quietly erode your confidence before you even begin.

So, let's name them and then let's put them down.

Myth 1: I'm not a natural salesperson.

This one appears early and frequently. Typically whispered. As if selling were some sort of personality trait – like being skilled at small talk or remembering birthdays.

But sales isn't something you're born with an innate knowledge of. It's a craft. And like any craft, it comprises various skills – listening, asking insightful questions, understanding needs and articulating value. Each of these can be learned, practised and improved.

If you've ever convinced someone to join your team, pitched to an investor or even explained why your product is important, you've already engaged in sales. You simply didn't term it as such.

Myth 2: If the product's good, it should sell itself.

This is the myth of meritocracy – that excellence alone will triumph. That if you create something sufficiently valuable, people will simply know.

However, in reality even the best solutions must be discovered, understood, trusted and purchased. This does not happen passively, particularly in B2B.

Your product may be excellent. However, your potential customer is busy, distracted and sceptical. They don't just require your solution; they need to feel that you understand their problem, that you can deliver and that choosing you won't expose them to unnecessary risk. Building that trust is essential in sales.

Myth 3: Sales means being pushy.

This is the image that many founders dread – the relentless, smooth-talking salesperson who won't accept no for an answer.

But the best salespeople don't push; they uncover, they ask, they listen and they guide. They don't force a sale that doesn't fit; instead, they help someone make a good decision – one that aligns with their goals.

You don't need to adopt a new personality to sell effectively. You don't need to become slick. You need to be clear, curious and credible.

Myth 4: I don't want to bother people.

This one is enveloped in politeness – something we Brits excel at. We don't wish to intrude. We don't want to impose. However, that instinct, while well-meaning, can prevent you from being present where you're needed.

If your product genuinely solves a problem, then your outreach isn't an interruption – it's an opportunity. You're providing a better way to accomplish something that matters. That's not disturbing people. That's being helpful.

Respect your prospect's time. Be considerate. Be succinct. But don't apologise for being.

Myth 5: I should wait until I'm ready.

This is perfectionism in disguise – waiting until the product is perfect, waiting until you have the right deck, the right script, the right logo.

However, sales is how you learn what 'ready' even looks like. It's how you refine your messaging, comprehend objections and discover what people truly care about.

You will never feel completely ready. That's not the goal. The aim is to start – and then improve – based on genuine conversations with real people.

A Quick Exercise: Sales Belief Audit

Spend five minutes noting the beliefs you currently hold about sales. Be honest. Then, beside each one, write a more constructive version.

Example:

- I'm not good at sales. → Sales is a skill I can learn.
- Selling is pushy. → Selling is about helping the right people make better decisions.
- I hate rejection. → Rejection is information. I can use it to get better.
  You're not attempting to become someone else. You're learning to perceive yourself – and sales – more clearly.

By unlearning these myths early, you grant yourself permission to sell in a manner that feels aligned, grounded and honest. That's the best place to begin.

Chapter one

THE MINDSET OF A SUCCESSFUL B2B SALESPERSON

'Whether you think you can, or you think you can't – you're right.' – Henry Ford

Welcome to the sharp end of the entrepreneurial journey – the stage where your big idea must face the marketplace. It's one thing to create a product or service you believe in: it's quite another to sell it. As the founder, that responsibility falls to you, whether or not you feel prepared.

Many founders, particularly those from technical or creative backgrounds, find themselves quietly dreading the moment they must sell. The very word 'sales' can conjure images of brash tactics, awkward conversations or the fear of rejection. However, successful founder-led selling doesn't require you to become someone you're not. Quite the opposite. It's about bringing more of who you are – your belief, your insight, your intent – to the table and doing so with structure and confidence.

Before you master techniques or perfect your pitch, you must address something more fundamental: your mindset. The beliefs you hold about sales, yourself and the role of a founder in driving commercial success will shape every interaction you have. Mindset isn't a soft skill; it's the foundation of everything that follows.

Sales As Helping

One of the most powerful mindset shifts you can make is to reframe sales as helping. If you perceive it as pushing, persuading, or convincing, you'll hesitate – and quite rightly so. However, if you view it as assisting someone in solving a problem or enhancing their business, your entire posture transforms.

Consider Tom, a first-time founder with an engineering background. He found sales uncomfortable – too performative, too transactional. However, once he began to view it as problem-solving, everything fell into place. In an early call, he bypassed the demo completely and devoted forty minutes to listening. At the end, the prospect expressed gratitude – not for selling but for aiding them in understanding their own internal inefficiencies. A week later, they signed.

This isn't a trick; it's a realignment. It's a decision to approach every sales conversation with curiosity, empathy and a genuine desire to create value.

Rejection and Resilience

Of course, even with the best intentions, you will still hear 'no'. Frequently. That's not a reflection of your worth or your product's potential. It's simply how B2B sales operates. Timing, budget and priorities – many factors are beyond your control. What you can control is how you respond.

Resilience serves as your emotional shock absorber. It enables you to recover from setbacks without losing momentum. It's not about being unaffected; it's about processing disappointment, extracting lessons and trying again.

Priya, the founder of an HR tech startup, transformed rejection into a visual process by creating a 'Rejection Wall' in her office. Each sticky note represented a lost deal, accompanied by a lesson she learned from it. Six months later, the wall was full and so was her first revenue milestone. 'Every "no" taught me something useful,' she said. 'That wall is how I built my pitch.'

The Founder Advantage

Founders possess a distinctive advantage in early sales. You know the product inside out. You comprehend the problem it addresses. You're profoundly invested in its success. Such conviction is difficult to feign – and equally challenging to resist. Buyers may not anticipate a polished salesperson from a startup but they value insight, authenticity and commitment.

When you present yourself authentically – not as a caricature of a salesperson – you foster trust. You create a genuine conversation. And that's what cultivates relationships in B2B.

Cultivating a Sales Mindset

Developing a strong sales mindset means embracing certain habits of thought:

- Belief in your value, your mission and your ability to learn.
- Curiosity about your customer's world, goals and challenges.
- Empathy for the pressures they face and the change they seek.
- Proactivity in starting conversations and following through.
- Resilience in the face of rejection or indifference.
- Focus on helping, not selling.

This isn't about pretending to be confident; it's about becoming competent and allowing confidence to grow from that.

KEY TAKEAWAYS

- Reframe selling as helping; it's about understanding problems and offering solutions.

- Your passion, insight and conviction as a founder are unique advantages.

- Rejection is normal – resilience, not perfection, is what counts.

- Curiosity and empathy open more doors than pushy sales tactics.

- Every call is an opportunity to refine your pitch and improve your offer.

FOUNDER'S FIELDWORK

Reframe Sales in Your Own Words: write down your own definition of 'selling' that aligns with helping and solving, not pushing. Pin it somewhere visible.

Conduct a 'Sales Belief Audit': list five beliefs you currently hold about sales. For each one, write a revised, empowering version (e.g. 'I'm not a natural salesperson', 'Sales is a learnable skill, just like product development').

Write down your biggest fear in sales. What would you say to a friend feeling the same?

Write Your Sales Purpose Statement: craft a one-sentence mission that defines why you're selling. ('I help [customer type] solve [problem] by providing [solution].')

Weekly Wins Wall: set up a visible space to track even the smallest wins (e.g. positive reply, improved objection handling). Reflect weekly.

Track Emotional Patterns: keep a journal for one week noting your emotional highs and lows related to sales activities.

Set a Founder Sales Block: schedule two ninety-minute weekly time blocks exclusively for outbound or customer-facing activity. Make it non-negotiable.

Chapter two

BUILDING UNSHAKEABLE CONFIDENCE AND RESILIENCE

'Success is not final, failure is not fatal: it is the courage to continue that counts.' – Winston Churchill

When you first start selling as a founder, it's easy to feel vulnerable. You're not merely offering a product, you're presenting something you have created; something you truly believe in. This connection makes rejection particularly painful.

Confidence and resilience form the emotional foundations of sustainable selling. However, they are not pre-installed; rather, they are developed through preparation, action and reflection.

Confidence through Clarity

Confidence doesn't mean being loud or slick. It means being clear – about what you offer, whom it helps and why it matters. That clarity is contagious. When you speak with conviction and coherence, people listen. They may not always agree but they'll take you seriously.

That clarity begins with doing the work. Know your product. Understand your customer. Prepare for meetings. Anticipate objections. When you've invested the time, you'll carry yourself differently – and prospects will sense it.

One founder I worked with, Alex, was terrified of calls. However, he prepared relentlessly – researching each company, rehearsing his pitch and mapping likely objections. After each call, he made notes and adjusted his approach. Within a month, he was leading conversations. The fear didn't disappear but it ceased to dominate the situation.

The Role of Resilience

Resilience is what keeps you going when your inbox is silent, your calls go unanswered and a guaranteed opportunity falls through. It's what helps you begin again tomorrow with the same energy.

Remember: sales is not a referendum on your worth. It's a process. Not everyone is ready, right or reachable. Your job is to continue learning.

If a conversation doesn't go well, ask yourself: what can I take from this? What might I try differently next time? Reflection transforms setbacks into fuel.

Building Habits That Support Confidence

- Create a 'Win Journal' – log three small wins each day.
- Set micro-goals – one call, one email, one meeting booked.
- Role-play regularly – rehearse key conversations with a peer or mentor.
- Develop a pre-call ritual – a moment to breathe, centre yourself and reconnect with purpose.
  These rituals are small, but they anchor you.

And don't go it alone. Sales can be lonely. Share the journey. Find other founders. Check in weekly. Celebrate progress together.

Redefining Rejection

Ultimately, rejection requires a reframe. It is not failure; it is information and feedback. At times, it even serves as protection – from an unsuitable client or a misaligned expectation.

Priya's Rejection Wall wasn't merely a clever morale tool; it served as a system for learning. Each 'no' had something to teach and over time those lessons transformed into revenue.

The goal is not to eliminate rejection. It's to lessen its sting, draw out its lessons and continue moving forward.

Final Thoughts

Confidence flourishes through clarity and repetition. Resilience develops through reflection and support. Both are skills. Both are trainable. As a founder, both will benefit you far beyond your early sales.

Selling may not be the job you envisioned. However, if executed properly, it will transform you into the leader your business requires.

KEY TAKEAWAYS

- Confidence comes from clarity – about your product, your purpose and your prospect.

- Rejection is not personal. Resilience is the skill of recovering and learning quickly.

- Consistent small wins build lasting momentum and self-belief.

- Sales is a craft – and like any craft, you can improve with honest feedback and practice.

- Your passion, preparation and presence make you the best person to sell your solution.

FOUNDER'S FIELDWORK

The Founder's Strength: write down three reasons customers should believe in you personally (e.g. industry insight, lived experience, speed of support). Keep this as your 'founder advantage reminder'.

Create a Win Journal: record three small wins at the end of each sales day, even if it's just sending one cold email or completing a tough call.

Role-Play Your Pitch: record yourself delivering your value proposition. Review it critically or ask a trusted peer for feedback.

List Rejection Reframes: note three recent rejections or objections and write what you learned from each. Treat them as data.

Prepare Power Rituals: choose a simple physical or mental ritual to centre yourself before sales calls (e.g. deep breath, posture check, repeat an affirmation).

Identify Your 'Sales Tribe': write down the names of three people you can connect with regularly for support and feedback on your sales journey.

PART 2

CLARIFYING WHAT YOU'RE SELLING

You can't sell effectively if your offer is unclear. This part helps you sharpen your understanding of what you do, who you assist and why it matters. You'll define your UVP, create a narrative that resonates, identify your ideal customers and discover what they're truly seeking – so you're not guessing when you hit the market.

Chapter three

DEFINING YOUR UNIQUE VALUE PROPOSITION (UVP)

'Marketing is no longer about the stuff that you make, but about the stories you tell.' – Seth Godin

What Makes You Different – and Valuable

So, you've got the right mindset developing and you're cultivating that inner steel of confidence and resilience. Excellent. Now, what precisely will you say when you stand before a potential B2B customer? You've created something you believe in but why should they have faith in it? Why should they select your nascent offering over established competitors, or even opt for doing nothing at all? The answer lies in your Unique Value Proposition or UVP. This isn't merely some elaborate marketing jargon; for a startup entrepreneur managing their own sales, it's the absolute foundation of every sales conversation you'll engage in.

Consider your UVP to be the shortest, clearest and most compelling answer to the question: 'Why should my business buy from you?' If you can't nail this, you're in for a tough slog. In the B2B world, where decisions are often complex and involve multiple stakeholders, a weak or vague UVP means you'll struggle to even get your foot in the door, let alone close a deal. And when you're a startup, with no established brand reputation and a product that might still have a few rough edges, your UVP must work even harder. It needs to cut through the noise and grab attention for all the right reasons.

One of the initial anxieties for entrepreneurs is defining a UVP when your product or service feels as though it's still being built, as if you're 'building the plane while flying it'. That's perfectly normal. Your early UVP doesn't have to be set in stone for all eternity. In fact, it will evolve. However, you need a strong starting point – a clear hypothesis about the value you offer – which you can then test and refine through those crucial early sales interactions. This chapter is about helping you forge that initial UVP, even while things remain in flux.

Let's break down the term 'Unique Value Proposition'. First up, 'Unique'. What does unique really mean, especially for a startup? It doesn't necessarily mean you have to have invented something that nobody else in the history of the universe has ever conceived. While true invention is fantastic, uniqueness in a business context can be more nuanced. It might be a unique combination of existing ideas, a novel approach to solving an old problem, or serving a very specific niche market that larger players overlook. While we're on the subject of niche products or services, do not feel that this is a sector you should devalue. Many niche products have gone on to make their founders and shareholders very wealthy; they often complete an offering from a bigger competitor and the competitor may go on to buy the niche company rather than develop their own product or service to enhance their own offering.

Your uniqueness could stem from your business model, your technology stack (if it genuinely offers a distinct advantage), your team's specific expertise or the highly personalised service you can provide as a smaller, more agile company. Perhaps you're quicker, more flexible, more focused, or you comprehend a particular industry's pain points with a depth that generic providers lack. As a founder, your passion and direct involvement can also serve as a unique selling point, especially in the early days. Don't underestimate the appeal of working directly with the visionary behind the solution.

Next, let's tackle 'Value'. This is the absolute core of your UVP. Critically, value is defined by the customer, not by you. You might be incredibly proud of a particular feature, but if it doesn't solve a significant problem, or create a tangible gain for your B2B customer, it holds little value for them. Your task is to get inside their heads and understand what truly matters to their business. Are you helping them make more money? Save money? Reduce risk? Improve efficiency? Become more competitive? Comply with regulations?

The value you offer can be quantified, such as 'reducing processing time by 30%' or 'increasing lead conversion by 15%'. These are invaluable, especially in B2B. However, in the early stages, some of your value may be less tangible – perhaps it's the strategic advantage of adopting new technology, the peace of mind from a more reliable service, or the ability to influence the product roadmap as an early adopter. Your UVP needs to articulate these benefits clearly. Always strive to translate your product's features into customer-centric benefits and, wherever possible, outcomes.

Finally, 'Proposition'. This means you're making a clear, concise promise. It's an assertion of the value you will deliver and the differentiation you offer. It's not just a statement; it's an offer, an invitation to engage further. It needs to be compelling enough to make a busy B2B professional stop and think, 'Hmm, that sounds interesting. I should learn more.' It's the hook that piques their interest. As the founder, you have a distinct advantage when it comes to defining your initial UVP. You have lived the problem you're trying to solve, or you have seen the opportunity with unparalleled clarity. Your deep understanding of the 'why' behind your venture is a powerful starting point. You're also on the front line, talking to those first potential customers. This direct feedback loop is invaluable. You can hear firsthand what resonates, what confuses and what problems they are truly grappling with. This allows you to iterate your UVP much faster than a large corporation with layers of bureaucracy. So, what are the essential ingredients of a strong UVP for a startup? While there's no magic formula, a good UVP typically addresses:

1. Your Target Customer: who, specifically, is this intended for? You cannot be everything to everyone. (We'll delve deeply into Ideal Customer Profiles in Chapter Five, but you need a basic understanding of this now.)

2. The Customer's Problem/Need: what significant pain point or unmet need are you addressing for this target customer?

3. Your Solution (Product/Service Name & Category): what is your offering?

4. The Key Benefit/Outcome: what is the single most important, tangible benefit your customer gets from your solution? How does it solve their problem?

5. Your Unique Differentiator: why you? What makes your solution distinct from the alternatives, including doing nothing or using a workaround?

I was told a fascinating story that illustrates just these points by a friend. He was working with a guy named Ben who launched a quoting tool for tradespeople but struggled to gain traction. His early pitch was vague: 'We help trades automate quotes.' Then he spoke to a veteran roofer he knew, who said, 'I hate wasting evenings pricing jobs I won't win.' That single sentence reframed Ben's UVP: 'We help roofers reclaim their evenings by sending faster, smarter quotes.' Within weeks, response rates jumped and conversions doubled. The best UVPs often start with a real customer's complaint.

The Clarity Test: Simple, Specific, Strong

Let's get practical. How do you, as a busy entrepreneur, begin developing your initial UVP, especially when resources are limited and your product might still be a 'minimum viable' version? Adopting a lean approach is essential.

Start by brainstorming customer pains. Don't just speculate. Engage with people in your target market. If you already have a few potential users or contacts, interview them. Ask open-ended questions. What are their biggest challenges related to the area your product addresses? What frustrates them about existing solutions? What are their aspirations? Listen more than you speak. You're searching for recurring themes, for problems that are urgent and which they are actively trying to solve.

Next, assess honestly your solution's current strengths. Given that your product or service is new and perhaps still evolving, what can it realistically accomplish well at present? Avoid overpromising based on future features. Concentrate on the core functionality that directly addresses one or two of the key customer pain points you've identified. It's better to be a robust solution for a narrow issue than a weak solution for a broad one.

Then, link those pains to gains. For each core strength of your solution, articulate how it enhances the customer's life or business in a tangible way. For instance, if your software automates a manual process (strength), the gain might be 'frees up 10 hours of staff time per week' (quantifiable benefit) or 'reduces errors and improves data accuracy' (qualitative but still strong benefit).

Take a quick, pragmatic look at your competitors. Who else is attempting to solve similar problems for similar customers? How do they present their value? Don't get bogged down in exhaustive competitive analysis at this stage (that's for Chapter Six). You're merely looking for their main selling points to identify gaps or areas where you can offer a different angle. Are they expensive and complex, whereas you're simple and affordable? Are they targeting large enterprises, while you're focused on the needs of SMEs?

Now, begin drafting multiple UVP statements. Don't strive for perfection on the first attempt. Experiment with different wording and try various angles. For example:

'We help [target B2B customer] solve [specific problem] by providing [your solution], which delivers [key benefit] unlike [competitor/alternative].'

'For [target B2B customer] struggling with [pain point], our [product/service] offers [primary benefit] by [how you do it differently].'

Remember to incorporate the 'Why You?' factor as a founder-led startup.

Your early customers might be taking a chance on a new company. What unique insight, commitment or advantage do you offer as the founder, deeply invested and directly involved? Perhaps it's your extensive industry expertise, your innovative approach unburdened by legacy thinking or your dedication to co-creating the ideal solution with your early adopters.

One of the most crucial steps for a startup is to test and iterate your UVP. Your initial draft is a hypothesis, not a sacred text. Every sales call, every email exchange and every demo presents an opportunity to test it. Does it resonate? Do the prospects' eyes light up (even metaphorically over the phone)? Do they quickly grasp what you do and why it matters? Or do you receive blank stares and perplexing questions?

Listen closely to the language your prospects use. How do they describe their problems? How do they articulate the value they perceive (or fail to perceive) in what you're offering? Often, they will provide the key phrases you need for your UVP. Be humble enough to adjust your messaging based on this real-world feedback. This iterative process is particularly vital when your product is still evolving. Your UVP may shift focus from one benefit to another as you gain insights into market needs and as your product capabilities develop.

There are several common pitfalls into which entrepreneurs stumble when defining their UVP. Being aware of these can help you sidestep them. A classic mistake is being too generic. 'We help businesses improve productivity' is a meaningless platitude. Which businesses? How? By how much? Get specific.

Another is focusing on features, not benefits. 'Our software has a cloud-based AI-driven dashboard' is a feature list. 'Our software gives you instant, actionable insights to cut operational costs by 15%' is a benefit-driven UVP. B2B buyers care about what your product does for them. Avoid making vague claims or using impenetrable jargon. If prospects need a dictionary to understand your UVP, you've already lost them. Simplicity and clarity are key. And while it's tempting, don't try to be everything to everyone. A UVP that appeals to everybody often truly excites nobody. Especially as a startup, focus is your friend. Being a big fish in a small pond is far better than being a minnow in an ocean.

Validation before Amplification

Resist the urge to assume you know what customers value. Your passion for your product is fantastic but it can create blind spots. Validate your assumptions by speaking to actual potential customers. And finally, as we have mentioned before, don't shy away from being niche. A sharply defined UVP for a specific target audience is far more powerful than a diluted one aimed at the masses.

The reality for many startups is that the product or service isn't 'finished' when you begin selling. This is where your UVP needs to be smart. You can focus on the core problem you solve exceptionally well, even if some bells and whistles are still on the roadmap. You can also frame the 'early stage' nature of your product as a benefit for the right kind of customer – the early adopter. These clients often value the opportunity to influence the product's development, to have their specific needs prioritised and to receive highly personalised attention from the founding team. Your UVP can incorporate this idea of partnership and co-creation.

Sometimes, especially with innovative or disruptive offerings, your UVP might also need to sell a vision. If you're creating a new category or challenging a deeply entrenched way of doing things, part of your value proposition is to paint a picture of a better future that your solution enables. This requires a balance between aspirational vision and concrete, near-term benefits.

To help you get started, here's a simple, widely used template you can adapt. It's often attributed to Geoffrey Moore in 'Crossing the Chasm', but the core idea is prevalent.

For [your target B2B customer segment]

Who [have a specific problem, need, or opportunity]

Our [product/service name] is a [category of solution] that provides [quantifiable key benefit or compelling reason to buy].

Unlike [the main competitor or current alternative],

We [state your key unique differentiator].

Let's imagine a startup creating project management software for small architectural firms. Their UVP might look something like this:

For small architectural firms with fewer than 20 employees who struggle to manage multiple client projects, deadlines and revisions efficiently, leading to overruns and client dissatisfaction, our 'ArchFlow' is a cloud-based project management platform that provides a simplified, visual way to track all project stages, communication and deliverables in one place, reducing administrative time by up to 25% and improving on-time project delivery. Unlike generic project management tools that are overly complex and expensive, or manual methods like spreadsheets and email, we are designed specifically for the unique workflows of architects, offering industry-specific templates and a focus on visual collaboration, all at an affordable price point for small firms.

This is a starting point. You should then test this. Do small architectural firms really see themselves in this? Is 'reducing admin time by 25%' believable and compelling? Is 'visual collaboration' the right differentiator? Only real-world feedback will tell you.

Do not get too hung up on filling in a template perfectly. The genuine value lies in the thinking process it prompts you to navigate. Who are you serving? What problem are you truly solving? How are you authentically better or different in a way that matters to them? Your UVP is not a static tagline you create once and forget. It is a living statement that will likely be refined many times, especially in the early days of your startup. As your product evolves, as you learn more about your customers and as the competitive landscape shifts, you should revisit and tweak your UVP to ensure it remains sharp, relevant and compelling.

Remember, the goal here isn't merely to have a UVP but to possess one that truly works – one that opens doors, sparks interest and clearly communicates why a B2B customer should take time out of their busy day to listen to a new entrepreneur offering a new solution. It serves as the foundation upon which you'll build your sales conversations, marketing materials and, ultimately, your customer base. Getting this right, even in its initial, evolving form, represents a significant step towards successful founder-led sales.

KEY TAKEAWAYS

- Your value proposition must clearly explain what you do, for whom and how it improves their business.

- Simplicity and specificity beat jargon and generalisation.

- The best propositions solve urgent problems and signal real outcomes.

- Don't guess – test your value proposition with real prospects.

FOUNDER'S FIELDWORK

The One-Sentence Test: write your proposition in one sentence: 'We help [customer type] who struggle with [problem] achieve [outcome] through [solution].'

Interview Three Target Customers: ask them about their pain points, current workarounds and what success looks like to them.

Translate Features into Benefits: list your top five product features. Write the direct benefit each delivers to your customer.

Talk to Ten: ask ten target customers to rate the clarity of your value proposition and summarise it back to you. Adjust based on confusion points.

Kill the Fluff: highlight all buzzwords in your current pitch and replace them with plain, punchy language.

Create Two Variants: draft one UVP for early adopters and one for more risk-averse mainstream prospects.

Chapter four

CRAFTING A COMPELLING VALUE PROPOSITION NARRATIVE

'People don't buy what you do; they buy why you do it.' - Simon Sinek

Turning Value into a Story

You've wrestled with your Unique Value Proposition (UVP) and pinned down what makes your offering special, whom it's for and the core problem it solves. That UVP statement serves as your compass. Now, how do you take that concentrated essence and transform it into something that truly captivates a potential B2B customer? The answer lies in narrative. This chapter is about moving beyond the what and why of your UVP to the how – how you communicate that value through a compelling story.

A UVP on its own, no matter how brilliantly defined, can feel somewhat like a list of ingredients. A value proposition narrative, on the other hand, is the full-course meal. It's the story you tell that brings those ingredients to life, making them appetising and memorable. In the often dry and data-driven world of B2B sales, a well-crafted narrative can be your secret weapon, especially as a startup founder. You're not merely selling a product or service; you're inviting someone into the story of their own potential success, with your offering playing a crucial supporting role.

Why does narrative work so well, particularly for an entrepreneur trying to gain traction? Stories connect with us on an emotional level. Even the most analytical B2B buyer remains human. A compelling story can bypass purely logical defences and create a deeper sense of understanding and connection. It simplifies complex ideas, making them easier to grasp and, importantly, easier to remember long after the facts and figures have faded. As a founder, you're uniquely positioned to be the chief storyteller. Your passion, your origin story and your deep understanding of the problem – these are all potent ingredients of narrative.

Consider this: when a prospect hears your story, they're not merely processing data points about your product. They're envisioning how their own business narrative might change for the better. They're picturing themselves overcoming current challenges and achieving their goals. This is far more persuasive than simply reciting a list of features. Your aim is to make your prospect the hero of this story, with your product or service as the trusty guide or powerful tool that helps them vanquish their villains (inefficiency, high costs, missed opportunities) and reach their treasure (growth, profitability, market leadership).

The Founder's Edge
So, what does a 'narrative' look like in a practical B2B sales conversation? We're not talking about spinning yarns or inventing fiction. We're discussing structuring your communication in a way that has a beginning, a middle and a satisfying (potential) end for the customer. A classic narrative arc in sales often involves highlighting a problem, agitating that problem so its impact is clearly felt, introducing your solution as the means to resolve it, showcasing the benefits of that resolution and providing evidence or proof.

The first step is to grab their attention with a compelling hook. You have precious few seconds to make an impression, especially with busy B2B decision-makers. Your hook needs to be relevant and intriguing. It could be a startling statistic related to their industry and the problem you solve. For example, 'Did you know that businesses like yours lose an average of X hours per week due to Y?' Or it could be a bold, benefit-driven claim drawn directly from your UVP: 'We help companies like yours cut their Z costs by up to 20% in the first six months.'

Another effective hook is a relatable mini-anecdote (perhaps drawing from the problem that inspired you to start your company) or a provocative question that makes them think about their current situation in a new light. 'What if you were able to onboard new clients twice as fast without increasing your team size?' The key is to tailor your hook. What keeps this specific type of prospect awake at night? Your initial understanding of your ideal customer profile, however nascent, will guide you here.

One of the best narratives I have heard was from the founder of a company in which I am personally invested. It is an electronic patient record system that resides in 'the cloud' and allows all records, results, scans and data about patients in the hospital to be stored in a single location, easily accessible for doctors. He began to build the product after a patient had to go through a procedure twice because a scan had been lost. The patient suffered a stroke when the procedure was repeated.

Once you have their attention, you need to delve into the problem or pain story. Your Unique Value Proposition (UVP) already identifies the core issue. Now, your narrative must develop it further, making it vivid and relatable. Don't merely state the problem; describe its symptoms, consequences and the frustrations it engenders. You want your prospect to nod along, thinking, 'Yes, that's exactly what we're dealing with.' Use empathetic language. Show that you understand their world and their struggles. You're painting a picture of their 'before' state – the current reality they're trying to escape.

For instance, instead of saying 'Our software solves inefficient workflows', you could say, 'Many firms we talk to find their teams are constantly switching between three different apps just to get a single project update. Key information gets lost in email chains, deadlines get missed because someone didn't see a critical comment and managers spend hours chasing status reports instead of focusing on strategic work. Does any of that sound familiar?' This helps them feel the pain, making them more receptive to a solution.

Now that the problem is clearly defined and its impact felt, you present your solution as the answer. This is where your product or service enters the narrative, not as the hero, but as the enabling tool or the wise guide. Transition smoothly from the problem to how your offering specifically addresses those pain points. Avoid a sudden, jarring shift into a feature dump. Instead, connect each relevant aspect of your solution directly back to the challenges you have just described.

If you mentioned information getting lost in email, you might say, 'That's precisely why we built [Your Product Name] with a centralised communication hub, so every conversation, file and approval related to a project lives in one accessible place.' You're not merely saying 'we have a communication hub' (feature); you're explaining why it matters in the context of their pain (benefit). Keep this part focused and concise, highlighting the elements of your UVP that are most relevant to this particular prospect or problem.

Next comes the most crucial part for the customer: the benefit/ transformation story.

This is where you paint the 'after' picture. What does their world look like once they've successfully implemented your solution? How is their business better? Focus on the tangible outcomes, the increased efficiency, the cost savings, the revenue growth and the reduced error rates. Quantify these benefits whenever possible, drawing from your UVP. 'Imagine reducing that administrative time by 10 hours a week. What could your team achieve with that extra capacity?' Don't forget the intangible benefits either: the reduced stress for their team, the improved employee morale, the enhanced reputation with their own clients and the peace of mind that comes from having a reliable system.

This is where you articulate the true value proposition – the positive change your solution brings. You're showing them the 'happily ever after' that's possible if they embark on this journey with you.

Throughout this narrative, you must seamlessly weave in your unique differentiator story. Why should they choose your startup and evolving product over established competitors or simply stick with their current imperfect workaround? Your UVP identifies what makes you different. Your narrative needs to illustrate why that difference matters. Perhaps your differentiator is your deep niche expertise. Your story might include how you, as a founder, experienced the exact same problem in their industry and built the solution you wished you had. It's how my friend with the electronic medical records company scores his biggest wins. If your differentiator is agility and customer focus as a startup, your narrative can highlight how early clients get to co-create the product and receive unparalleled support directly from the founding team. 'Unlike generic platforms that try to be everything to everyone, we focused solely on [their industry/problem], which means every feature is designed with your specific workflow in mind.' Don't just state your uniqueness; tell a brief story that demonstrates its value.

Structure That Sells

To make your narrative truly compelling, several techniques can be employed. Analogies and metaphors are fantastic for simplifying complex ideas, especially if your product is technical. If your software streamlines a convoluted process, you might compare it to a fast track lane at a theme park. This makes the benefit instantly understandable.

Utilise customer language. As you engage with more prospects and refine your UVP, pay close attention to the words and phrases they use to articulate their pains and desired outcomes. Incorporating this language into your narrative makes it resonate more deeply. It demonstrates that you are listening and that you 'get' them. It reinforces your credibility within their industry.

Keep it concise and clear. B2B buyers are notoriously short on time. Avoid corporate buzzwords, technical jargon (unless you are certain your audience is highly technical and appreciates it) and rambling explanations. Get to the point. Every sentence should serve a purpose in advancing the narrative. Think of it like a movie trailer – it needs to be engaging and convey the essence of the story quickly.

Embrace the 'show, don't just tell' principle. Instead of merely asserting that your solution saves time, briefly illustrate how. This could be a mini-case study (if you have one). Even if you're pre-revenue, you can use a hypothetical yet realistic example: 'Imagine a typical client onboarding. Right now, it takes you X steps and Y days. With our system, you could automate steps A, B and C, cutting that down to Z days. For an average of five new clients a month, that's a saving of...' If appropriate, a very quick demo of the one key feature that delivers the core value can be exceptionally powerful.

Visual storytelling isn't just for pitch decks. Even in a verbal conversation, use words that help your prospect visualise the benefits. 'Picture your team dashboard at the end of the month, all green, all projects on track...' This helps make the abstract benefits more concrete.

And, as always, your passion and authenticity as the founder are tremendous assets. Allow your genuine belief in your solution and sincere desire to help the customer to shine through. Your story is inherently more credible because you're not just a hired salesperson; you're the architect of this vision. Don't hesitate to share a brief and relevant part of your own journey if it helps build connection and underscores your commitment.

It's also crucial to understand that your value proposition narrative isn't a one-size-fits-all monologue. You need to adapt it for different contexts and audiences.

The elevator pitch is your narrative distilled into its purest, most potent form: 30–60 seconds to convey the core problem, your solution, the key benefit and your uniqueness. This is for those fleeting networking opportunities or brief introductions. One of the best salespeople I ever knew always ended his elevator pitch with a simple question: 'Does that sound like something you would benefit from?'

In an initial sales call or meeting, you have more time to expand the narrative. You can make it more interactive, pausing to ask questions, gauge understanding and tailor the story in real-time based on their responses. Here, your narrative framework guides the conversation rather than dictating a script.

When it comes to written communication, such as introductory emails or proposals, the narrative must be adapted for the medium. An email may begin with a powerful hook and a concise problem/benefit statement, aiming to secure a conversation in which you can tell the fuller story.

A proposal often includes a dedicated section reiterating the client's challenges (showing that you've listened) and then detailing how your solution addresses them, focusing heavily on the benefits and ROI.

For pitch decks, the narrative structure is often very explicit. Slides may follow a sequence such as: The Problem, Our Solution, How it Works, Why Us (Differentiation), The Benefits/Value, Market Opportunity, Team and Call to Action. Each slide contributes a chapter to the overall story.

Just like your UVP, your narrative is not static. It is a living entity that should be iterated upon using a lean approach. Your initial version is a hypothesis. Test it constantly. In every sales interaction, observe what resonates. Where do prospects lean in? What makes their eyes light up? What questions do they ask? Where do you sense confusion or disengagement? This feedback is invaluable.

Utilise it to refine your language, reorder your points or even adjust the core focus of your story. Perhaps you discover that a benefit you thought was secondary is actually the primary driver for your target audience. Alternatively, the way you're explaining your differentiator may not be clear. Be prepared to tweak, rewrite and retest. Your narrative will evolve as your product matures, as you gain more customer proof points and as your understanding of the market deepens. The story you tell to attract visionary early adopters (who might be excited by the novelty and the chance to influence development) may need to shift when you target more pragmatic mainstream buyers (who seek proven results and stability).

To put this into action, try this practical exercise: take a piece of paper or open a new document and outline your core value narrative. Don't aim for perfection; just note the key elements.

1. The Hook: what's your most compelling opening line or question for your ideal customer?
2. The Problem Story (the 'Before'): briefly describe the main pain point(s) your ideal customer faces, in their language. What are the consequences?
3. Your Solution (the 'Bridge'): how does your product/service directly address this problem? Focus on one or two core aspects.
4. The Benefit/Transformation Story (the 'After'): what are the top three tangible outcomes or positive changes a customer can expect? How does their situation improve?
5 Your Unique Differentiator Story (the 'Why You'): what's the key reason they should choose you over any alternative and what's a brief story or example that illustrates this?

Once you have this basic framework, practise telling this story. Tell it to yourself, tell it to a colleague, tell it to a mentor. The more comfortable you become with your core narrative, the more naturally and persuasively you'll be able to deliver it. Remember, you're not just conveying information; you're sparking imagination and building belief. Your value proposition narrative is the vehicle that carries your UVP into the hearts and minds of your future customers, turning prospects into partners.

KEY TAKEAWAYS

- Narratives are more persuasive and memorable than product lists.

- A great story connects emotionally and logically with your ideal customer.

- Use real-world examples or anecdotes to build credibility and trust.

- Structure matters – guide the prospect through a journey of understanding.

FOUNDER'S FIELDWORK

Write Your Origin Story: in one hundred and fifty words, no more, explain why you started this business and the problem you're solving.

Build that Five-Part Sales Narrative:
  Hook
  Pain story
  Solution
  Transformation
  Differentiator

Design a Demo Script: create a five-minute walkthrough of your product that highlights how it solves a key customer pain.

Create a Visual Analogy: think of a metaphor that simplifies your solution (e.g. 'Slack is like a digital office watercooler').

Practice in the Mirror: deliver your full narrative out loud. Aim for clarity and confidence, not perfection. Better still, record it and have a peer critique it for you.

Chapter five

UNDERSTANDING YOUR IDEAL CUSTOMER PROFILE (ICP)

'If you market to everyone, you market to no one.' – Meredith Hill

Finding Your Focus

All right, let's talk about aiming. You wouldn't go hunting (metaphorically speaking, of course) with a blindfold on, spraying pellets in every direction and hoping for the best, would you? Well, selling without a clear idea of who you're selling to is essentially the same thing. You'll waste a colossal amount of your most valuable startup resources – time, energy and the little cash you might have – and end up with a multitude of near misses and frustration. This chapter is all about removing that blindfold by helping you define your Ideal Customer Profile, or ICP. This is ground zero for effective B2B sales, especially when you're the founder, the chief cook and bottle-washer and, now, the lead salesperson.

Your ICP is essentially a detailed portrait of the ideal customer for your product or service at this moment. It's not about who could theoretically use your offering in a utopian future where you possess unlimited resources. Instead, it focuses on identifying the specific type of business and the individuals within it that are the best fit for what you can provide today, particularly as a new enterprise. Consider it a description of the customer who will not only purchase from you but also find success in using your solution, feel satisfied with their purchase and, ideally, spread the word about you. For an entrepreneur just starting out, this clarity is not merely a nice-to-have; it's crucial for survival and early growth.

Many first-time entrepreneurs, brimming with enthusiasm for their new creation, fall into the trap of thinking, 'My product is so great, everyone will want it!' While that optimism is admirable, it serves as a precarious starting point for your sales strategy. Attempting to be everything to everyone often results in being nothing special to anyone. Your marketing messages become diluted, your product development is pulled in too many directions and your sales efforts lack focus. As a lean startup, you simply do not have the luxury of such a scattered approach. You need to place your bets wisely. Remember that compelling value proposition and narrative we worked on in the previous chapters? Your ICP is the audience whom that narrative is specifically designed to captivate.

Your UVP answers, 'Why should they buy from you?'; your ICP answers, 'Who is they?' And here's a crucial point for any founder feeling the pressure of an evolving product: your first ICP is a hypothesis. It's your best educated guess based on your current knowledge. You will test it, learn from it and undoubtedly refine it. That's the lean way. Don't wait for perfect clarity; start with a good hypothesis and begin validating.

So, why is laser-focusing on an ICP so critical from the moment you decide to make your first sale? Firstly, it's about resource efficiency. As a founder, your time is arguably your most valuable asset. Pursuing prospects who are a poor fit is a surefire way to waste that time with little to show for it. A clear ICP helps you concentrate your limited sales and marketing budget (which might be zero initially) where it will yield the most impact. Every email you write, every call you make and every networking event you attend (even virtually) should be guided by your ICP.

Secondly, your early customers are not merely sources of revenue; they are essential sources of product development feedback. If you attract customers who genuinely fit your ICP, their feedback will be incredibly relevant for refining your product or service in a manner that enhances its core value. Conversely, feedback from unsuitable customers can divert you down rabbit holes, creating features that your ideal users don't actually require, pulling your offering away from its core strengths.

Thirdly, a well-defined ICP allows for messaging resonance. Once you know precisely whom you are addressing – their specific industry, their challenges, their goals – you can tailor your value proposition narrative (Chapter Four) to speak directly to their reality. Generic messaging is overlooked; targeted messaging captures attention. Your communication becomes sharper, more relevant and infinitely more persuasive because it feels as though it was crafted just for them.

This targeted approach naturally leads to higher conversion rates. When you converse with the right people about the issues they genuinely care about and offer a solution that's a suitable fit, you're far more likely to advance them through your sales process. You'll spend less time attempting to convince sceptics who were never a good match in the first place and more time engaging genuinely interested prospects.

Moreover, early success with customers who fit your ICP helps you build crucial traction and compelling case studies. A satisfied, successful customer who embodies your ideal profile is the best marketing asset a startup can possess. Their testimonial, their story of how you assisted them, becomes powerful social proof that attracts other similar customers. This is how you begin to build momentum from zero.

And let's not forget the advantage of founder-led sales. As the visionary behind the product, you often possess a deep, intuitive understanding of the problem you're addressing. This insight can be invaluable in identifying those initial ideal customers. You have lived the pain or observed it clearly. Leverage that unique perspective to recognise others who share that same experience.

Attributes That Define Your Best Customers

When discussing your initial ideal customers, particularly for a startup, we need to be far more specific. Not just any paying customer will suffice. You're searching for a specific type. These trailblazers will be:

Acutely experiencing the pain. The problem your solution addresses isn't a minor inconvenience for them; it's a significant headache. They feel it daily or weekly and it has tangible negative consequences for their business.

Aware of the pain and actively seeking solutions. They not only have the problem but know they have it and, critically, they're likely already looking for ways to solve it or are at least open to new approaches. This means they're more receptive to hearing about your offering.

Equipped with the budget (or able to champion finding it). Even if your solution is incredibly affordable, there's always a cost, even if it's just the time to implement. In B2B, this means understanding their purchasing authority or their ability to influence those who hold the purse strings.

Early adopters or innovators. These are businesses or individuals within businesses who are more willing to take a chance on a new, unproven solution from a new, unproven company. They are less risk-averse and often gain satisfaction or competitive advantage from being first.

Possessing the potential for advocacy and referrals. You want your first customers to be so thrilled with the results that they become enthusiastic advocates, providing testimonials, case studies and referrals to other similar companies.

Manageable to service. As a lean startup, you can't afford to have your first few clients be so demanding or complex that they consume all your resources. Look for customers whose needs you can realistically meet and exceed with your current capabilities.

Able and willing to provide quality feedback. Your first customers are your co-creators. You need them to be articulate about what's working, what's not and what they'd like to see improved. Their insights are pure gold for your product iteration.

Here it's worth noting an entrepreneur I know named Sarah. Sarah secured a meeting with a national retailer just two months after launching her supply chain visibility platform. She went above and beyond to meet their requirements, exhausting her team, postponing product updates and resulting in no outcomes – they ghosted her after six weeks. That painful lesson redirected her focus towards mid-sized manufacturers who had urgent needs and could make quick decisions. Within three months, she closed her first five deals. 'Just because a whale's in sight doesn't mean it's your meal,' she told her audience, of which I was part, about a year later.

Use Data and Conversations, not Guesswork

So, how do you, the busy founder, actually sit down and define this initial ICP, especially when you're building from scratch and possibly don't have a wealth of existing customer data to analyse?

Your first step is to revisit the problem that your product or service addresses. We discussed this when defining your UVP. Now, delve even deeper. Who, specifically, experiences this problem most acutely? What are the common characteristics of businesses or individuals who struggle with this particular challenge? If your software automates a specific type of financial reporting for a certain industry, then that industry immediately becomes a key component of your ICP.

Consider your 'why'. Why did you start this company in the first place? Were you attempting to solve a problem you personally encountered in a previous role or industry? If so, individuals resembling your former self, in companies akin to your previous employer, could constitute your initial ICP. Your own experience and empathy for their situation provide you with a significant advantage. Next, let's gather some more structured data. For B2B sales, we focus on firmographics – these are descriptive attributes of the companies themselves:

Industry/Vertical: be as specific as possible. 'Technology companies' is too broad. 'Early-stage B2B SaaS companies with a focus on subscription billing' is far better. Why this industry? Do they have specific compliance needs that you address? Unique workflows? A particular competitive landscape?

Company Size: this can be measured by annual revenue, the number of employees or even the number of customers. Are you targeting small local businesses, mid-market companies or (less likely for an initial ICP for a startup) large enterprises? Company size often correlates with the complexity of their needs, their budget and their decision-making processes. As a startup, you might find more traction initially with Small to Medium-sized Enterprises (SMEs), who are often more agile and open to innovative solutions from smaller vendors.

Geographic Location: are you targeting businesses locally, regionally, nationally or internationally? Consider your ability to service them. Early on, focusing locally or within your own country might be more manageable.

Company Structure/Maturity: is it a startup, a family-owned business, a rapidly scaling company or a more established, stable entity? This can influence their willingness to adopt new technologies and the speed of their decision-making.

Existing Technology Stack: if your product integrates with or replaces specific technologies, understanding what your prospects currently use is vital. For example, 'Companies currently using HubSpot CRM but needing more advanced sales automation features.'

Beyond the company itself, it is essential to comprehend the individuals within those companies – the decision-makers, influencers and users. This involves examining psychographic and behavioural data:

Job Titles/Roles: who is the person most likely to feel the pain your solution addresses? Who holds the authority to make the purchasing decision? Who will be the primary user? In B2B, it's rarely a single individual. You might encounter an economic buyer, a technical buyer and end-users, each with distinct concerns. Identify these key personas. For instance, if you sell marketing automation software, your ICP might include the 'Marketing Manager', the 'VP of Sales' (who benefits from better leads) and perhaps even the 'CFO' (who approves the budget).

Their Goals and Motivations: what are they aiming to achieve in their role? What does success entail for them? Are they driven by revenue targets, cost reduction, efficiency gains, career advancement or innovation? How can your solution assist them in realising their personal and professional goals?

Their Challenges and Frustrations: beyond the specific problems your product addresses, what are their other daily headaches? Understanding their broader context fosters empathy and allows you to position your solution more effectively.

Their 'Watering Holes': from where do these individuals obtain their information? What industry publications do they read? What conferences (virtual or physical) do they attend? Which LinkedIn groups or online forums are they active in? Knowing this is invaluable for low-cost lead generation and targeted outreach later.

Their Buying Process: how do companies like this typically evaluate and purchase solutions in your category? Is it a swift decision by one person or a protracted, committee-based process? Understanding this helps you navigate the sale.

Their Tolerance for Risk and Attitude Towards New Solutions: are they innovators or early adopters, or are they more cautious and prefer proven solutions? This will significantly influence how you position your startup and your product.

Just as important as knowing who is your ideal customer, is knowing who isn't. Define your Negative ICPs. These are the types of businesses or individuals who are a definite poor fit. They might be too large for you to service effectively, too small to afford even your lowest tier, in the wrong industry where your solution offers little value or simply have needs that are wildly different from what you provide. Identifying them clearly helps you avoid wasting time and resources on dead-end leads. Saying 'no' to the wrong prospects is just as crucial as saying 'yes' to the right ones.

Now, all this may seem like a considerable amount of research, particularly when you're a solo founder attempting to develop a product and manage all other aspects. The good news is that for your initial ICP, you can utilise low-cost or no-cost research methods:

Leverage Your Network: this is often your richest, most accessible resource. Talk to friends, former colleagues, mentors and anyone else in your professional circle. Describe what you're building and the problem it solves. Ask them, 'Who do you know that experiences this? What kinds of companies are they in?' You'd be surprised how willing people are to help and make introductions.

Founder's Intuition and Experience: don't discount your own gut feeling, particularly if your startup was born from your direct experience in a specific industry. You already possess a wealth of tacit knowledge about the people and companies in that space.

Analyse Early Inquiries (If Any): if you've already received a few tentative enquiries or sign-ups (perhaps from a basic landing page), scrutinise them. What do these early hand-raisers have in common? What are their industries, company sizes, job titles? This is real-world data, no matter how small the sample size.

'Ideal Customer' Interviews: this is perhaps the most powerful technique. Identify a handful of individuals (5–10 is a great start) who you believe might fit your tentative ICP. Reach out and request a brief (15–20 minute) informational interview. Crucially, do not attempt to sell them anything in this initial conversation. Your goal is solely to learn. Prepare open-ended questions like:

Can you tell me about your role and key responsibilities? What are some of the biggest challenges you face in [area related to your solution]? How are you currently dealing with [the problem your product solves]? What does your process look like for evaluating and purchasing new tools/services like this? Where do you typically look for information about new solutions in your industry?

Listen attentively. Take thorough notes. You might consider offering a small token of appreciation for their time, such as early access to your product, a future discount or simply your heartfelt gratitude.

LinkedIn Research: LinkedIn is an absolute goldmine for B2B ICP research. Utilise the search filters to find individuals with specific job titles in your target industries and locations. Examine their profiles: what skills do they list? What type of content do they post or engage with? What groups are they members of? This can provide you with valuable insights into their professional lives and priorities. Even the free version of LinkedIn is incredibly useful for this; Sales Navigator offers more advanced capabilities if your budget allows.

Online Communities and Forums: where do your potential ideal customers gather online? This might include industry-specific forums or associations, subreddits, Quora topics or professional association groups. Lurk and learn. What questions are they asking? What frustrations are they expressing? What solutions are they discussing? This is akin to eavesdropping on your target market's candid conversations.

'Competitor Lite' Analysis: take a quick look at companies offering similar or adjacent solutions. Who are they explicitly targeting on their website? What kinds of customers are featured in their testimonials, case studies or client logos? This can provide clues about viable market segments. (We'll dive much deeper into formal competitive analysis in Chapter Six.)

Reflect on Your 'Best' Past Professional Relationships: if you have prior business or work experience, consider the clients or colleagues with whom you worked best. What characteristics did they share? Why was the relationship successful? These past positive experiences can sometimes indicate the types of people or organisations with whom you would thrive as an entrepreneur.

Once you've gathered this initial information, document your ICP. Don't simply keep it floating around in your head. Writing it down makes it concrete and shareable (even if it's just with yourself initially or future team members). You don't need a fifty-page report; a simple one-page document or slide will suffice. Consider using a straightforward template. You could structure it like this:

Ideal Customer Profile: [Assign a memorable name to your ICP, e.g. 'Sarah the SaaS Marketing Manager']

Industry/Vertical: [e.g. B2B SaaS]

Company Size (Revenue/Employees): [e.g. $ 2m–$10 M ARR, 20–100 employees]

Location: [e.g. North America]

Specific Characteristics: [e.g. Actively using HubSpot, seeking to enhance lead nurturing]

Persona (Key Contact – e.g. Marketing Manager)

Job Title(s): [e.g. Marketing Manager, Head of Demand Generation]

Key Responsibilities: [e.g. Lead generation, campaign management, content creation]

Goals/Motivations: [e.g. Increase MQLs by 20%, improve conversion rates, demonstrate ROI of marketing spend]

Biggest Challenges/Pain Points (related to your solution): [e.g. Spending too long on manual reporting, struggling to personalise outreach at scale, low engagement with current content]

Watering Holes (where they get info): [e.g. MarketingProfs, HubSpot Blog, specific LinkedIn groups, SaaS-focused podcasts]

Common Objections/Concerns (especially about a new startup): [e.g. Will you be around in a year? Is your product mature enough? Can you integrate with X?]

Buying Process Insights: [e.g. Decisions typically involve the Marketing Manager and VP of Sales; evaluation period ~45 days; looks for peer reviews and case studies]

Why They'd Choose Us (Our UVP for them): [Link back to how your unique value proposition specifically benefits *this* ICP]

Negative ICP Markers: [e.g. Companies < £ 1M ARR (can't afford/too small), enterprise clients (>500 employees – too complex for us now), businesses not using a CRM]

Giving your ICP persona a name, such as 'Sarah the SaaS Marketing Manager' or 'Tech-Startup Tom' makes it more tangible and easier to visualise when crafting messages or making sales decisions. Always remember to include a note: Version 1.0 – Subject to Revision!

With your initial ICP documented, no matter how imperfect, you can begin using it to guide your early sales efforts. This isn't merely an academic exercise; it's intensely practical.

Focus Your Outreach: knowing your ICP informs you where to invest your valuable time searching for leads. If Sarah, the SaaS Marketing Manager, frequents specific LinkedIn groups, you'll know where to be. If she participates in certain industry webinars, you'll know which ones to prioritise.

Tailor Your Messaging: your value proposition narrative (Chapter Four) can now incorporate language, examples and pain points that resonate deeply with Sarah. You're no longer shouting into the void; you're engaging in a relevant conversation.

Qualify Leads More Effectively: when a new inquiry arises, or when you meet someone at an event, you can swiftly evaluate them against your ICP criteria. Are they a good fit? If yes, fantastic! If not, you can politely disengage or, if appropriate, refer them to someone else. This approach saves both you and them considerable time. Don't attempt to force a square peg into a round hole. Sadly, not all revenue is good revenue; sometimes the cost of acquiring it, or the longer-term damage it can cause, makes it 'bad revenue'.

Inform Product Development: the feedback obtained from these carefully selected ideal early customers is invaluable. It will guide your product roadmap, assisting you in building features that truly matter to your target market, rather than allowing distractions from requests by outliers.

Finally, and this is crucial for the lean sales approach, comprehend the iterative nature of your ICP. Your initial definition is your best guess, a starting hypothesis. As you embark on your sales outreach and engage in genuine conversations with prospects – both those who purchase and those who don't – you will gain an immense amount of insight.

Continuously ask yourself: did this customer (or prospect) fit my documented ICP? If yes, what did I learn from our interaction that reinforces or refines the profile? Did they mention a pain point which I hadn't considered? Did they use specific language I should adopt? If no, why did I win them (if I did)? Or why did I lose them? Does this imply my ICP is too narrow, too broad or perhaps focused on the wrong segment? Are there adjacent customer segments that appear particularly interested, even if they don't perfectly align with my current ICP? Could this represent a new opportunity?

Don't be afraid to tweak, adjust or even completely pivot your ICP if the data and your experiences suggest doing so. This isn't a failure; it's agile selling at its best. As your product evolves, your company grows and the market changes, your ICP will likely evolve too. The key is to remain curious, keep listening to the market and be willing to adapt. Gaining a clear understanding of whom you're selling to is the foundational step that makes every subsequent sales activity more effective and efficient.

KEY TAKEAWAYS

- Focused targeting enables sharper messaging and shorter sales cycles.

- Your ideal customer is one who has the problem, feels it acutely and is ready to act.

- ICPs should evolve in response to market feedback and client performance.

FOUNDER'S FIELDWORK

Draft Your ICP Profile: include industry, company size, role/title of buyer, key pains and existing tools they use.

Create a Negative ICP List: write down three types of customers who shouldn't buy from you – and why.

Conduct Five Customer Discovery Calls: ask target customers about their roles, pain points and decision processes.

Build a LinkedIn Target List: identify ten people who match your ICP. Note their job title, company and any shared connections.

Complete a One-Page ICP Sheet: create a printable or digital version you can refer to before every outbound campaign.

Chapter six

MARKET RESEARCH AND COMPETITIVE ANALYSIS

'The goal is to out-listen your competition.' – Bernadette Jiwa

Why Research Fuels Sales Insight

Right then, you've wrestled with your Ideal Customer Profile (ICP) and have a decent picture of 'Sarah the SaaS Marketing Manager' or 'Manufacturing Mike'. You know who you want to talk to. Fantastic. But Sarah and Mike don't live on a desert island. They exist in a bustling marketplace, filled with noise, other vendors, existing solutions and their own set of industry pressures. To effectively sell to them, you must understand that world. This chapter is about rolling up your sleeves and doing a bit of detective work – market research and competitive analysis, startup style.

Now, I can already hear some of you thinking, 'Market research? Competitive analysis? I'm a solo founder trying to build a product, answer support emails and remember to eat! I don't have time or money for fancy reports and corporate espionage!' And you're absolutely right to think that way if your image of this involves commissioning expensive studies or hiring consultants. But that's not what we're discussing here. For an entrepreneur just starting out, market research and competitive analysis are not about boardroom presentations; they are gritty, street-smart tools for survival and discovering your unique edge. They're about understanding the game before you place your bets.

Think of it this way: your ICP tells you who the fish are. Market research helps you understand the pond they swim in – how big is it, what are the currents and are there any regulatory sharks? Competitive analysis helps you identify the other anglers – who else is fishing for Sarah and Mike, what bait are they using and how can you offer something more enticing? Without this knowledge, you're essentially casting your line into the dark, hoping for a bite. With it, you can be much more strategic, efficient and ultimately successful in your sales efforts. This isn't about spending resources you don't have; it's about intelligent, focused investigation using the resources you do have: your brain, your internet connection and your ability to talk to people.

Firstly, let's get a grip on the 'market'. This term can seem vast and daunting but for your purposes it's about defining your realistic operational area, particularly in these early stages. Your Unique Value Proposition (Chapter Three) and your Ideal Customer Profile (Chapter Five) have already accomplished much of the groundwork here. If your UVP pertains to providing, say, a hyper-efficient invoicing tool for freelance graphic designers, then your market isn't 'all small businesses' or even 'all freelancers'. It's specifically the segment of freelance graphic designers who feel the pain your tool alleviates.

Consider the geographical scope. Are you initially targeting local businesses, national ones or (ambitiously, but possible with digital products) international from the outset? What specific industry niche are you concentrating on? Is your solution customised for a particular problem that only certain types of business face? The more specific you are, especially as a startup with limited resources, the easier it is to focus your efforts and make an impact. Attempting to conquer 'the global market for software' on day one is a recipe for exhaustion. Strive to be a big fish in a small, well-defined pond first.

Forget those hundred-page market research reports that cost more than your first year's revenue projections. As a founder, you need 'directional accuracy' and a sense of viability. Is this pond you've chosen big enough to sustain your business and its growth ambitions? Is it a thriving ecosystem or is it drying up?

Here are some lean ways to gauge this:

Google Trends: a simple yet powerful tool. Enter keywords related to the problem you solve or the type of solution you offer (e.g. 'project management for architects', 'sustainable packaging suppliers'). Observe how interest has trended over time. Is it growing, stable, or declining? You can also compare different terms to see which resonates more.

Basic Keyword Research: tools like Google Keyword Planner (you will need a Google Ads account but you don't have to spend money on ads to use it for research) or the free tiers of tools like Ubersuggest or Moz Keyword Explorer can provide insight into how many people are searching for terms related to your offering. High search volume for a problem doesn't automatically indicate a great market but it does demonstrate awareness and active searching for solutions.

Industry Associations and Trade Publications: many industry bodies publish annual reports or statistics, often with free summaries available. Trade magazines and websites frequently discuss market trends and challenges. A quick search for '[Your ICP's Industry] market size' or '[Your ICP's Industry] trends' can unearth useful nuggets.

Public Company Data: if there are large, publicly traded companies that serve a broader segment of your market, their annual reports or investor presentations (often found in the 'Investor Relations' section of their websites) can contain overviews of market conditions and future outlooks.

'Bottom-Up' Estimation: this serves as a sanity check. If your ICP is 'small architectural firms with 5–20 employees in the UK', endeavour to determine approximately how many such firms exist (LinkedIn Sales Navigator can be beneficial for this if you have access or you might find government business statistics). Then, estimate what percentage you could realistically capture over time. Does that number seem worthwhile? The goal is not to pinpoint a precise figure down to the last decimal point. It's about building confidence that there is a genuine need and a sufficiently large group of potential customers for your solution.

Listening for Market Pulse: Trends, Pains and Opportunities. Beyond just size, you must understand the dynamics of your market. What are the prevailing winds? What are the current significant conversations, frustrations and emerging needs? This is where you put your ear to the ground.

Your ICP's Watering Holes: remember those places where 'Sarah the SaaS Marketing Manager' gathers her information (Chapter Five)? You should be there too, not (yet) to sell, but to listen. Subscribe to the key industry newsletters she reads. Follow the thought leaders and relevant company pages she follows on LinkedIn. Tune in to the podcasts she listens to. What topics keep arising? What new challenges are being discussed?

Online Communities: subreddits related to your ICP's industry or role, specialised Facebook groups, Quora topics and niche forums can be goldmines. People often share their unfiltered frustrations and seek advice in these spaces. You will witness real problems being discussed in authentic language.

The 'Job To Be Done' (JTBD) Framework: this concept encourages you to consider what your customer is fundamentally trying to achieve when they 'hire' a product or service. People do not buy a drill bit simply because they want a drill bit; they buy it because they want a quarter-inch hole. They are purchasing outcomes. Grasping the underlying 'job' your ICP aims to fulfil can uncover a broader market context and highlight opportunities for innovation. For instance, if your software aids with project reporting, the JTBD might be 'demonstrate progress to stakeholders' or 'ensure projects stay on budget'. This broader perspective can assist you in recognising market needs that existing categories of solutions do not address.

Quick Sanity Checks: Economic and Regulatory Winds. You don't need to become an economist but having a cursory awareness of major economic shifts or significant regulatory changes that could impact your target market is sensible. For instance, if your product assists businesses in complying with a new data privacy law, that law acts as a massive market driver. Conversely, if your ICP is in an industry severely affected by an economic downturn, they may be tightening their belts, which will influence their willingness to invest in new solutions. A quick glance at major business news headlines or relevant government agency websites for your niche should suffice to alert you to any significant red flags or green lights.

Competitive Analysis: Sizing Up the Other Players (Even if They're Just Spreadsheets). All right, you've gauged the pond. Now, let's examine the other anglers. Competitive analysis may seem like something only large companies with dedicated departments do, but for you, the founder, it's crucial to know who else is attempting to solve your ICP's problem. Everyone Has Competition. Yes, Even You. Many entrepreneurs, especially those who've created something genuinely innovative, tend to think, 'We have no competitors!' As an angel investor, I have heard this statement a thousand times in pitches. I can usually identify one in less than five minutes using Google. Therefore, with the utmost respect, that's rarely the case. Even if no one provides the exact same solution as you, your ICP is currently addressing their problem somehow or they wouldn't be in business.

Your competition includes:

Direct Competitors: companies offering a similar product or service to your ICP. These are typically the ones that come to mind first.

Indirect Competitors: these address the same core problem but with a different approach or a different type of solution. If you provide project management software, an indirect competitor might be a consultancy firm that assists in managing projects or even a highly skilled administrative assistant who does it all manually. For early stage startups, these indirect competitors are often more significant than you may realise.

The Status Quo/Inertia: this is often your biggest competitor, particularly with a new or disruptive offering. It's easier for a prospect to do nothing, stick with their current (even if inefficient) way of operating or muddle through with spreadsheets and email, than it is to take a risk on a new solution from a new company. Your research needs to equip you to overcome this inertia by clearly demonstrating the cost of not changing. Ignoring these forces is akin to stepping into a boxing ring without knowing whether your opponent is a featherweight or a heavyweight champion.

Learning from Competitors (without Copying Them)

Here are some scrappy techniques for competitor intel (no cloak and dagger required). You don't need a trench coat and dark glasses for this. Most of the information you need is publicly available or can be gleaned through keen observation.

Website Deep Dive: this is your first and most obvious stop. Scrutinise their website. What is their stated UVP? Who do they say their target audience is (compare it to your ICP)? What features and benefits do they highlight? Do they publish pricing? Examine their case studies and testimonials – what kinds of customers are they showcasing? What topics do they cover on their blog (this indicates their areas of claimed expertise)? Even their 'Careers' page can be revealing; showing what roles they're hiring (e.g. 'Salesforce developers' tells you something about their tech stack or focus).

Social Media Sleuthing: check their LinkedIn, Twitter, Facebook, Instagram (whatever is relevant for their industry). What kind of content do they post? How do they engage with their audience? Crucially, what are people saying to them and about them in comments or replies? Look for both praise and complaints.

Review Sites Are Your Friends: platforms like G2, Capterra, TrustRadius, Software Advice (for software) or industry-specific review sites can be incredibly insightful. Real users often leave detailed reviews outlining pros, cons and their overall experience. Look for recurring themes – what do customers consistently love or hate about them?

Become a 'Prospect' (Ethically and Observantly): sign up for their email newsletters. This allows you to see their marketing messaging and cadence. Attend their public webinars. Observe how they present their product, what questions attendees ask and how they are handled. If they offer a free trial or a freemium version of their product, try it out. Get a feel for their user experience, their onboarding process and the core functionality. The aim here is not to deceive or steal trade secrets. It's to understand their offering and sales process from an external perspective, just as any genuine prospect would. If you ever feel uncomfortable, err on the side of transparency.

Your Prospects and Customers Are Your Best Intel Source: this is perhaps the most valuable and direct method. When you're talking to your ICP (during those initial ICP interviews from Chapter Five, or your early sales conversations), don't be afraid to ask, 'What other solutions or approaches have you considered for tackling [the problem]?' 'Have you looked at [Competitor X]? What were your thoughts?' 'What do you like or dislike about the way you're currently handling this?' Listen carefully to their answers. They'll tell you who they see as alternatives and what their perceptions are. This is real-time, highly relevant competitive intelligence.

What to Look For: Building Your Competitive X-Ray Vision. As you gather this information, what should you focus on?

Their Product/Service Offering: what are the core features? What are their main strengths? More importantly, what are their perceived weaknesses or gaps, especially in relation to the needs of your ICP? Don't just create an extensive list of features; strive to understand the value each feature is meant to deliver.

Their Pricing and Business Model: how do they structure their pricing? Is it a monthly/annual subscription, a one-off fee, usage-based or freemium? Is their pricing transparent and easily accessible, or must you engage with sales? How does their pricing appear to compare to the value they provide and how would it contrast with what you plan to offer?

Their Marketing and Sales Approach: how are they reaching their customers? Are they focused on content marketing and SEO? Do they run many paid ads? Are they active on social media? What is the tone of their sales messaging – is it aggressive, consultative or technical?

Their Stated UVP and Positioning: how do they distinguish themselves in the market? What unique claims do they make? Do their marketing and product genuinely support these claims?

Customer Perception and Reputation: what do reviews and social media comments indicate about their reputation? Are they viewed as innovative, reliable, expensive, difficult to use or having great support?

The Simple Startup Competitive Matrix.

To avoid drowning in data, create a straightforward method to organise your findings. A simple table can work wonders. Don't strive for an exhaustive dossier on every potential competitor. Begin with the 2–3 most relevant ones – those who are directly targeting your ICP or addressing the same pressing problem.

You can create a simple table for your notes:

Competitor Name

Their Stated UVP Focus

Competitor A e.g. 'All-in-one platform for large enterprises'

Their Target Audience (vs. your ICP) e.g. Fortune 500 companies, complex needs

Perceived Key Strengths e.g. Feature-rich, established brand

Perceived Key Weaknesses/Gaps (Opportunities for You!) e.g. Too complex and expensive for SMEs, slow to innovate, poor support for smaller clients.

Competitor B (Indirect – e.g. Manual Spreadsheets) N/A (It's a workaround) Anyone trying to manage the problem manually

Free (initially), highly flexible, error-prone, time-consuming, doesn't scale, no collaboration features, no insights

Pricing Model (if known/estimable) e.g. high-tier subscription, long contracts N/A (Cost is in wasted time/errors)

How We Can Win/Our Key Differentiator Against Them e.g. 'We're nimble, affordable and laser-focused on the specific needs of SMEs like [Your ICP]. Simpler to use, faster to get results.' 'We automate what you're doing manually, saving you X hours/week and reducing errors, allowing you to focus on core business activity.'

Add more rows as needed...

Keep this matrix lean and focused on actionable insights. It's a working document, not a historical archive. The 'How We Can Win' column is where the rubber meets the road – it compels you to think strategically.

Spotting Gaps, Trends and Customer Language

This research isn't merely for intellectual curiosity; it serves as fuel for your sales engine. Here's how to convert your newfound market and competitive understanding into tangible sales advantages:

Sharpening Your Axe: Refining Your UVP and Messaging. Armed with insights about what your market truly values and how competitors are (or aren't) meeting those needs, you can now revisit your UVP (Chapter Three) and your value proposition narrative (Chapter Four). Is your differentiation clear enough? Does your messaging directly address the gaps you've identified in competitors' offerings? For instance, if you discover that all your competitors are targeting large enterprises and your ICP is a small business owner, your UVP and narrative should scream 'Built for small businesses like yours!'

Spotting the Gaps: Identifying Your Niche and Opportunities. Your research might reveal underserved segments within your broader market or specific pain points that competitors are completely overlooking. These gaps are your openings! Perhaps everyone is focused on one industry, while an adjacent industry with similar problems is being ignored. Maybe existing solutions are all too complicated and there's a clear need for simplicity. These insights enable you to fine-tune your ICP and tailor your outreach to where you have the highest chance of resonating.

Sooner or later, particularly in B2B, a prospect will say, 'We're also looking at [Competitor X]' or 'How are you different from [Well-known Incumbent]?' Your competitive analysis is your preparation for this moment. You don't want to criticise your competitors – it appears unprofessional and insecure. Instead, you want to confidently and knowledgeably articulate your unique advantages in relation to the prospect's specific needs. A good response might be: 'Yes, Company X offers a solid solution, particularly if your main priority is [something they do well]. However, we find that clients like you, who are specifically focused on [a need your solution excels at], prefer our approach because [your key differentiator and its benefit to them].'

Understanding how competitors price their offerings, and the value they provide for that price, will be crucial when defining your own pricing strategy (which we'll cover in more detail later). Similarly, observing which marketing channels your competitors use successfully (or unsuccessfully) can inform your own lead generation efforts (Chapters 13–18). You might choose to compete directly in a channel where you believe you can excel or you might identify channels they are neglecting where you can establish your presence.

KEY TAKEAWAYS

- Research helps you identify patterns, gaps and opportunities others miss.

- Your customers' language is more valuable than your competitors' marketing.

- Competitor awareness should inform, not dictate, your approach.

FOUNDER'S FIELDWORK

Identify Your Top Three Competitors: list what they do well, where they fall short and how you differ. Write down their top three messages, pricing strategy (if known) and positioning.

Fill in a Competitive Matrix: create a four-column table: Feature/ Your Startup/Competitor A/Competitor B.

Gather Voice-of-Customer Insights: read ten competitor reviews (e.g. on G2, Capterra, Reddit) and highlight recurring complaints or desires.

Spy Tactfully: sign up for your competitors' newsletters, trials or webinars to understand their messaging and positioning.

Craft a 'Why Us?' Comparison Slide: prepare a simple visual you can use during pitches that articulates your key advantage.

PART 3

FINDING AND ENGAGING BUYERS

Equipped with clarity, it's time to connect with prospects. This section addresses the practical aspects of engaging your market – from active listening and persuasive communication to prospecting, content creation, cold outreach and networking. It's about building meaningful relationships, not merely filling a pipeline. Selling commences with conversation.

Chapter seven

THE ART OF ACTIVE LISTENING IN B2B SALES

'Most people do not listen with the intent to understand; they listen with the intent to reply.' – Stephen R. Covey

Listening as a Competitive Advantage

All right, let's discuss a skill that is so fundamental yet often overlooked, particularly when you're a passionate entrepreneur eager to share your brilliant new product or service: listening.

It sounds almost too simple, doesn't it? 'Of course, I listen!' you might say. But there's a world of difference between passively hearing what someone says and truly, actively listening.

For a founder navigating the tricky waters of early B2B sales, active listening isn't just a nice-to-have; it's a bona fide superpower. It is the key to unlocking customer needs, building trust when your brand is unknown and gathering the crucial feedback that will shape your offering.

Many entrepreneurs, fuelled by understandable enthusiasm for their creation, can inadvertently dominate sales conversations. They are so keen to explain all the wonderful features and benefits that they forget the prospect has a story to tell, a problem to outline and needs that must be understood before any solution can be effectively proposed.

If your sales 'conversations' feel more like monologues delivered by you, then this chapter is your friendly intervention. We are going to delve into the art and, yes, the practical science of active listening, specifically tailored for you, the founder who needs to make every interaction count.

So, what exactly is this 'active listening' we speak of and how does it differ from merely not talking?

Active listening is not simply pausing your own stream of thought long enough for the other person to finish their sentence so you can jump back in with your pre-prepared points. It's not about impatiently waiting for that tiny gap where you can unleash your perfectly crafted pitch. It's a conscious effort to hear, understand and retain the information being conveyed by the speaker. It involves engaging with what they're saying on multiple levels, not just processing the words.

Think of it this way: passive hearing is like having the radio on in the background. You might catch snippets, but you're not truly absorbing the content. Active listening, on the other hand, is like tuning into your favourite podcast with the intent to learn something specific or to deeply understand the host's perspective. It requires focus, presence and a genuine desire to grasp the message being sent, both explicit and implicit. It's about understanding the meaning behind the words, not just the words themselves.

One common pitfall, especially when you're under pressure to make a sale, is to spend the time the prospect is talking formulating your rebuttal or planning your next brilliant statement. Your mind races ahead, thinking, 'Okay, when they finish this point, I'm going to tell them about feature X and then I'll counter with benefit Y.' While they're speaking, you're essentially in a mental waiting room, just biding your time. This isn't listening; it's rehearsing an internal monologue.

Furthermore, active listening isn't about hearing one keyword related to a problem your product solves and then immediately pouncing with your solution. 'Ah, you said "inefficient workflow"? Well, let me tell you all about our amazing workflow automation tool!' Hold your horses. While your enthusiasm is commendable, jumping in prematurely often means you're offering a solution before you've fully grasped the contours of their specific problem, its impact on their business or what they've already tried. This can make you seem pushy or, worse, as though you're not interested in their actual situation.

At its core, active listening is driven by genuine curiosity. As a founder, you should be intensely curious about your potential customers. What are their biggest headaches? What are their aspirations? How does their business really work? What challenges are they facing that perhaps even they haven't fully articulated? This curiosity is especially vital when your product is new and your understanding of the ideal customer is still evolving. Every conversation is a treasure trove of insights, but you need the key of active listening to unlock it.

The Structure behind Great Listening

Now, let's break down the mechanics. How do you actually practise active listening in a B2B sales context, particularly when you're a busy entrepreneur, possibly taking calls from a less-than-ideal office environment? First and foremost is paying full attention. This sounds obvious, but in our hyper-distracted world, it's a real skill. This means more than just not browsing social media while you're on a call. It means mentally minimising all the other tasks clamouring for your attention – the product bug you need to fix, the investor email you need to draft, the lunch you haven't had time for. For those crucial minutes you're with a prospect, they need to be your universe.

If you work from a home office or a noisy co-working space, take practical steps to minimise interruptions. Put a sign on your door, silence your phone notifications (all of them!), close unnecessary browser tabs and inform anyone else in your space that you're on an important call. Anything that can divert your focus away from the prospect is an enemy of active listening.

Your ability to truly concentrate is fundamental.

When you're on a video call, or in those rarer early-stage in-person meetings, your non-verbal cues play a significant role in conveying attention. Maintain appropriate eye contact (look at the camera on video calls, not just their image on your screen). Nod to show understanding. Your posture can also signal engagement – leaning in slightly often indicates interest. These subtle signals inform the speaker that you're focused and value what they're saying.

Ultimately, paying full attention is about achieving mental focus – being truly present in the conversation. It involves consciously setting aside your internal chatter and dedicating your cognitive resources to understanding the person you're speaking with. This isn't easy, especially when you're juggling a multitude of startup priorities, but it's a discipline worth cultivating.

Next is demonstrating that you are listening. It's not enough merely to listen; the prospect needs to feel heard. This entails providing subtle feedback that encourages them to continue and reassures them that their message is being received. Think of it as providing the 'green lights' in a conversation. Simple verbal affirmations like 'uh-huh', 'yes', 'I see', 'that makes sense' or 'tell me more about that' can be very effective. These aren't interruptions; they're small interjections that signal you are following along and are engaged with their narrative. They serve as conversational oil, keeping the dialogue flowing smoothly.

On video calls, as mentioned, body language is key here as well. A thoughtful nod, a raised eyebrow to indicate interest or surprise, or a smile when appropriate – these visual cues reinforce your attentiveness. Even without a visual, your tone of voice when you offer those brief affirmations can convey your level of engagement.

The third critical component, which truly distinguishes active from passive listening, is providing feedback and clarifying. This is where you engage actively with the content of what is being said to ensure mutual understanding. It's akin to a checkpoint in the conversation.

One of the most powerful techniques here is paraphrasing. This involves restating the prospect's key points in your own words. For example, 'So, if I understand correctly, the biggest challenge you're facing with your current system is its inability to scale during peak demand, which leads to costly downtime. Is that right?' This serves two purposes: it confirms your understanding and demonstrates to the prospect that you were genuinely listening and processing what they said.

Similarly, summarising can be quite effective, especially after a prospect has explained a complex issue or a series of points. You might say, 'Okay, so just to recap, the main issues we've discussed are the lack of integration between your sales and marketing platforms, the difficulty in obtaining accurate reports and the significant amount of manual data entry your team is doing. Have I captured the main challenges?' This ensures you're both on the same page before moving forward.

Don't hesitate to ask clarifying questions. If a prospect uses jargon that you don't understand or makes a statement that's somewhat vague it's perfectly acceptable to ask for further detail. 'Could you tell me a bit more about what you mean by "streamlining your client onboarding"?' or 'When you say "integration challenges", what does that specifically look like for your team on a day-to-day basis?' Open-ended questions (those that cannot be answered with a simple 'yes' or 'no') are particularly useful here, as they encourage the prospect to elaborate. For a founder, these clarifying techniques are incredibly important. Your prospects are discussing their world, their problems and their needs. Your understanding of these needs is still developing, especially if your product is also evolving. Ensuring you accurately grasp their situation prevents you from making incorrect assumptions that could derail the entire sales process.

The fourth element is deferring judgment. This means listening with an open mind, without immediately jumping to conclusions or mentally (or verbally) critiquing what the prospect is saying. It's about absorbing their perspective before overlaying your own.

As an entrepreneur, you are deeply invested in your solution. It is easy to hear a problem and immediately think, 'My product can fix that!' However, deferring judgment means allowing the prospect to fully articulate their pain points, their current situation and perhaps even their frustrations with past solutions, without interrupting in order to correct them or offering your fix prematurely.

This also means being open to hearing things that might challenge your assumptions about your product or market. A prospect might describe a need that your 'baby' doesn't currently meet or express a concern which makes you uncomfortable. Resist the urge to become defensive. Instead, listen with the intent to understand their perspective. This feedback, even if it's difficult to hear, is invaluable for a startup.

Avoid imposing your solution before they've fully articulated their picture. If you jump in too early with how your product is the perfect answer, you might miss crucial details about their needs that could lead you to position your product suboptimally or, worse, realise later it's not a good fit after all.

Finally, we have responded appropriately. This is where your active listening pays off by enabling you to tailor your response directly to what you've heard. Your contribution to the conversation is now informed and relevant. Instead of launching into a generic pitch, you can now address their specific points, acknowledge their concerns and demonstrate that you've understood their unique context. 'You mentioned that your team is struggling with X and Y; our clients who've faced similar issues have found that Z feature really helps them by...'

Showing empathy is also a key part of an appropriate response. 'I can see how frustrating it must be to deal with those system crashes during your busiest periods.' Acknowledging their challenges on a human level helps build rapport and shows you're not just a vendor trying to make a sale but a potential partner who understands their plight.

Crucially, the timing of introducing your solution is paramount. Only after you've truly listened, clarified and understood their needs should you begin to explain how your product or service can specifically help them. Your pitch then becomes a natural extension of the conversation, directly addressing the pain points they've already articulated.

From Surface Symptoms to Root Causes

So, why go to all this effort? What are the tangible benefits of mastering active listening for you, the founder-salesperson? They are numerous and significant.

Firstly, you'll uncover hidden needs and deeper pains. Prospects often don't lead with their most significant or deeply felt problem. They might describe surface-level symptoms. For example, a prospect might say, 'We need better reporting.' Through active listening and clarifying questions, you might discover that the real, underlying pain is, 'Our CEO wastes hours every Monday morning trying to manually consolidate data from three different spreadsheets, because our current reports are unusable, and it's impacting strategic decision-making.' That's a much more compelling problem to solve.

Active listening is also foundational for building rapport and trust. When people feel genuinely heard and understood, they are much more likely to trust the person they are speaking with. As a startup founder with potentially no established brand reputation, building this trust quickly is absolutely vital. Listening well is one of the quickest ways to achieve this. It demonstrates respect and makes the prospect feel valued. You will also receive direct product feedback and insights to refine your UVP and ICP on the fly.

Every sales conversation is a research opportunity. As prospects describe their problems, listen to the precise language they use – you can then incorporate this into your own messaging. They might highlight aspects of your (or a competitor's) offering that they particularly value or dislike, providing you with clues about which features to prioritise or how to position your product more effectively. Their reactions to your questions can assist you in sharpening your ideal customer profile.

Furthermore, active listening helps you identify their true buying motivations. People buy for their own reasons, not yours. By listening intently, you can pick up on the emotional drivers, the key business objectives or the personal wins that motivate their search for a solution. Is it about saving money, reducing risk, gaining a competitive edge or perhaps even looking good to their boss? Understanding these underlying motivations helps you tailor your persuasion. From a purely practical standpoint, active listening can save you valuable time and resources. By quickly and accurately grasping a prospect's needs and assessing whether they are a good fit for your offering, you avoid wasting time on lengthy presentations of irrelevant features or, worse, pursuing deals that were never going to close. Misunderstandings are time-consuming; active listening minimises them.

Now, how can you, the busy entrepreneur, hone these listening skills without adding another significant task to your already overflowing plate? One powerful yet simple technique is to embrace the power of intentional silence. Don't feel the need to fill every pause in the conversation. When a prospect finishes speaking, or after you ask a question, wait a few seconds before responding. This gives them a chance to add further thoughts (often, the most valuable insights come after a brief pause) and it allows you a moment to process what you've heard.

Develop a system for quick and effective note-taking during calls. You don't have to transcribe the entire conversation. Instead, jot down keywords, key pain points they mention, important metrics, questions they ask and any action items. This not only aids your memory but also demonstrates your attentiveness if you refer back to their specific points later. For a founder, these notes also provide valuable data for product development and refining sales strategy.

Before each sales call or meeting, set a clear listening intention. For example: 'During this call, my primary goal is to understand their current process for managing X and the three biggest challenges they face with it.' Having a specific listening goal helps to focus your attention and guides your questions.

Perhaps one of the biggest challenges for passionate founders is overcoming the urge to interrupt with your brilliant solution. You hear a problem and your mind screams, 'I can fix that!' Train yourself to consciously hold back. Make a mental note (or a quick written one) of the point you wish to make, but allow them to finish. Channel your passion for your product into an equally fervent curiosity about your customer's world.

Finally, remember that active listening isn't merely a standalone technique; it's the foundation for so many other critical sales skills. The insights you gain from genuinely listening will make your persuasive communication (Chapter Eight) far more targeted, help you identify leverage points in negotiations (Chapter Nine), build stronger rapport (Chapter Ten) and enable you to understand and handle objections with grace and expertise (Chapter Eleven). Mastering the art of active listening is an investment that will yield dividends throughout your entire B2B sales journey.

KEY TAKEAWAYS

- Active listening builds trust and reveals opportunities your competitors may miss.

- Don't just hear – interpret, validate and clarify.

- The better your diagnosis, the stronger your proposal.

FOUNDER'S FIELDWORK

Use the Seventy/Thirty Rule in Conversations: record one sales call and track your talk time vs. the prospect's. Aim for thirty percent founder, seventy percent customer.

Prepare Five Discovery Questions: draft open-ended questions that explore pain points, goals and current tools.

Practice Reflection Techniques: after your next conversation, paraphrase what the customer said to confirm your understanding.

Create a 'Do Not Pitch' Timer: for your next discovery call, set a ten-minute timer before you're allowed to talk about your product.

Ask 'What Else?' Three Times: during a needs discussion, follow up three times to deepen your insight into the customer's situation.

The Three-Second Rule: pause for three seconds after a prospect speaks. Let them fill the silence – often with gold.

Listening Log: after each call, write down three things the customer said that surprised you or shifted your understanding.

Chapter eight

MASTERING PERSUASIVE COMMUNICATION TECHNIQUES

'The single biggest problem in communication is the illusion that it has taken place.' - George Bernard Shaw

Influence without Manipulation

So, you've spent time honing your active listening skills, as we discussed in the previous chapter. You're now better equipped to truly understand your B2B prospect's needs, pains and motivations. That's a substantial step. However, understanding is only half the equation. The other half involves responding in a way that not only addresses those needs but also gently and effectively persuades them that your fledgling solution is the right answer. This chapter focuses on mastering the art of persuasive communication – not as a means of manipulation or high-pressure tactics, but as a way to clearly, confidently and compellingly articulate the value you, as a founder, bring to the table.

For many entrepreneurs, particularly those from a technical or product background, the notion of 'persuasion' can feel a bit uncomfortable, perhaps conjuring images of slick salespeople. But let's reframe this. Persuasive communication, especially in founder-led B2B sales, centres around education and alignment. It's about helping your prospect see the connection between their problem and your solution. It's about building a bridge of understanding and trust. Your goal isn't to strong-arm anyone; it's to guide them to a logical conclusion that benefits their business. As a founder, your innate passion and deep knowledge, when communicated effectively, are incredibly persuasive assets.

The beauty of being a founder is that your persuasive communication can be deeply authentic. You're not merely reciting a script prepared by a marketing department; you're speaking from the heart, from a place of genuine belief in what you've built and the problem it solves. This chapter will provide you with practical techniques to channel that authenticity into compelling messages that resonate with B2B buyers, helping you transition from a tentative first conversation to a confident step towards a sale, even when your brand is unknown and your resources are limited.

At the very foundation of persuasive communication lies clarity and simplicity. B2B decision-makers are invariably busy individuals. They are bombarded with information daily. If your message is convoluted, filled with jargon or fails to get to the point swiftly, you'll lose their attention faster than a free trial sign-up during a system outage. Your product or service might be technically complex, but your explanation of its value doesn't have to be. Think clear, concise and compelling.

One of the biggest traps for founders is the 'Curse of Knowledge.' You live and breathe your product. You understand every nuance, its technical architecture and its subtle brilliance. The problem is, your prospect doesn't. They are starting from scratch. You must consciously step out of your expert mindset and into their shoes. Avoid industry acronyms they might not know, or the internal 'startup-speak' that makes sense to your small team but is meaningless to an outsider.

A good rule of thumb is the 'explain it to your grandma' test (or any intelligent person outside your specific field). If you can articulate what you do and why it matters in terms they can easily grasp, you're on the right track. This isn't about dumbing down your message; it's about making it accessible. Simplicity is a sign of deep understanding, not a lack of sophistication. It shows respect for your prospect's time and cognitive load. Always remember the golden rule of sales communication: WIIFM, or 'What's In It For Me?' Your B2B prospects aren't interested in your product's features for their own sake; they care about what those features can do for their business. We touched on this when defining your UVP but it bears repeating in the context of ongoing communication. Every time you talk about an aspect of your product or service, you need to mentally connect it to a tangible benefit or outcome for them.

For example, instead of saying, 'Our software has a real-time analytics dashboard,' which is a feature, you'd say, 'Our real-time analytics dashboard means you can immediately see how your campaigns are performing, allowing you to make faster, data-driven decisions and stop wasting budget on what isn't working.' See the difference? The first is informative; the second is persuasive because it highlights a clear benefit and addresses a potential pain point (wasted budget, slow decisions). Strive to use strong action verbs and, wherever possible, quantify the benefits. 'Increase sales by 15%', 'reduce processing time by 30%' or 'cut onboarding costs in half'. Numbers are powerful persuaders in the B2B world. Even if you're an early-stage startup without extensive case studies, you can often use reasonable estimates based on your product's capabilities or industry benchmarks, always being transparent about your assumptions.

The Power of Framing and Language

The way you frame your message can significantly impact how it's received. Framing is about presenting information in a specific context to influence perception. It's not about misrepresenting facts but about highlighting the aspects that are most relevant and appealing to your prospect. For example, you could frame your solution as a way to 'gain a competitive advantage' or 'avoid falling behind competitors'. Both might be true, but one might resonate more depending on the prospect's mindset.

One powerful psychological principle in framing is loss aversion. Research shows that people are often more motivated to avoid a loss than to achieve an equivalent gain. Therefore, instead of simply stating, 'Our solution will help you save X amount, you could frame it as, 'Right now, you might be losing Y amount each month due to inefficiency Z; our solution helps you stop that loss.' This must be handled ethically and based on a genuine understanding of their situation, but it can be very effective.

Another framing technique is anchoring. The first piece of information presented often acts as an anchor, influencing how subsequent information is perceived. If you're discussing pricing, for example, the initial figure mentioned can set a reference point. You can also employ the contrast principle. By showing how your solution compares favourably to a more expensive, more complex or less effective alternative (even if that alternative is just their current manual process), you can make your offering appear more appealing.

We discussed crafting your value proposition narrative in Chapter Four. Now, let's consider how to effectively deliver stories as a persuasive communication technique. Humans are wired for stories. Facts and figures are often forgotten, but a good story remains. As a founder, you possess a wealth of material: your own journey of identifying the problem, the 'aha!' moment that led to your solution, or even early (anonymised if necessary) anecdotes of how your product is beginning to help people.

Your founder's origin story can be particularly compelling for a startup. It humanises your business, explains your 'why' and builds an emotional connection. It doesn't need to be an epic saga; a concise, authentic account of the problem you observed and why you became passionate about solving it can be very persuasive. 'I used to struggle with this exact issue in my previous role and I knew there had to be a better way, which is why I built...'

You can also use mini-stories to illustrate specific benefits or to make a point more relatable. Instead of merely stating that your customer support is excellent, you could share a brief, true story about how you or your team went the extra mile for an early user. A simple structure for such a mini-story is: Problem (the customer faced this), Struggle (it caused this difficulty), Solution (we did this), Outcome (and here's the positive result).

Active listening (Chapter Seven) focuses on understanding. Strategic questioning builds on this by using questions to guide the prospect's thinking and help them realise for themselves why your solution is a suitable fit. This approach is far more persuasive than simply telling them. Instead of making a statement, you can often phrase it as a question that leads them to the same conclusion.

For example, instead of saying, 'Our solution will save you a lot of time,' you might ask, 'If you could automate tasks X, Y and Z, how much time do you estimate that would free up for your team each week?' Or, after they've described a significant problem, you could pose an implication question like, 'What's the likely impact on your Q4 targets if this issue isn't addressed soon?' These questions encourage them to reflect and articulate the value in their own terms.

Good strategic questions are open-ended and thought-provoking. They can help prospects uncover needs they hadn't fully realised or quantify the impact of their current problems. Be careful to avoid questions that feel like an interrogation or leading questions that come across as transparently self-serving. The goal is to foster a collaborative exploration, with you as the knowledgeable guide.

Clarity, Confidence and Call to Action

As a founder of a new company, establishing credibility and projecting confidence (without veering into arrogance) is paramount. Your prospects are taking a risk on an unknown entity. Your communication style can either reassure them or amplify their concerns. Begin with your verbal delivery.

Speak clearly, at a moderate pace and endeavour to minimise filler words like 'um', 'uh' and 'you know'. Recording yourself while practising your pitch can be excruciating but incredibly helpful for identifying these verbal tics.

Your tone of voice matters immensely. It should convey enthusiasm, conviction and professionalism. Even if you're nervous (which is perfectly normal!), aim for a tone that sounds assured and knowledgeable. When discussing your product or the problem it solves, your deep understanding as the founder is a significant asset. Allow that expertise to shine through, but always frame it in terms of how it benefits the customer.

Non-verbal communication is equally crucial, especially in video calls or any face-to-face interactions. Maintain good eye contact (with the camera during video calls). Sit or stand tall; good posture conveys confidence. Use natural gestures to emphasise points, but avoid fidgeting. These cues, often subconscious, significantly contribute to the prospect's perception of your credibility and trustworthiness.

One of the biggest challenges is often the 'newness' factor. How do you confidently address concerns about being a startup? Don't hide it, frame it. 'Yes, we're a newer company, which means we're incredibly agile and our early clients like you get direct access to the founding team and have a real opportunity to shape our product roadmap. We're deeply committed to the success of every single one of our early partners.' Preparation is essential here – anticipate these concerns and have confident, positive responses ready.

In B2B sales, you rarely sell to a single individual. Decisions are often made by a committee or, at the very least, involve multiple stakeholders, each with different priorities and perspectives. A technical lead will care about integration, security and ease of use. A finance manager will focus on ROI, cost savings and contract terms. A department head might be concerned with strategic alignment and team productivity. Your persuasive communication must be tailored accordingly.

Before a key meeting involving multiple stakeholders, endeavour to understand who will be present and what may be their likely concerns. During the conversation, be prepared to adjust your emphasis. When addressing the technical expert, you may delve deeper into the relevant technical aspects. When the CFO raises a question, pivot to the financial benefits and the business case. This does not mean altering your core message but rather highlighting the facets of your value proposition that resonate most with each individual.

For instance, to the CFO, you might emphasise, 'By automating these manual processes, our clients typically see a reduction in operational costs of around X%, leading to a payback period of Y months.' To the end-user manager, you might say, 'The feedback we get most often from teams using the platform is how much it simplifies their daily workflow and reduces frustration, allowing them to focus on more strategic tasks.'

Whilst discussing persuasive communication and the way businesses make buying decisions, it is important to pause here. One essential aspect is finding out what the approval process is within a business. How and who decides what they buy? During the sales interaction, it is crucial to discover this. I have seen many examples where salespeople are convinced a sale is complete only for it to stall at the contract-signing stage because not everyone involved in the decision-making process is aligned or convinced. Your job is to prevent this. It is quite permissible, as the sales process continues (and it is a process, remember), to ask that question. 'Could you tell me what your decision-making process is and who needs to be involved and onboard?' If they mention someone in the chain who is senior and you have not yet spoken to them, the easiest way to address this initially is to offer help. 'Is there anything you need that will help the process, possibly a summary I could prepare for you to show X detailing our business and the costs and benefits of implementing our solution?' Persuasive communication is all about multiple touch points and you want to create advocates among the people to whom you are physically talking. Most of the sales process occurs when you are not present, so you want to ensure that the people who wish to buy from you become your sales team within their own business.

Building belief is crucial when you lack a long list of marquee clients or years of market presence. How can a startup incorporate proof? It requires creativity and leveraging what you do have. If you have beta testers, their (permissioned) feedback, even if informal, can be powerful. 'Our early beta users in [their industry] have told us that feature X has been a game-changer for them.'

Your own founder's expertise and story can serve as a form of proof. 'I spent ten years as a [role relevant to the problem] and experienced this exact challenge firsthand, which is why I designed this solution to specifically address…' You can also use analogies to established concepts to make your innovative solution more comprehensible and less risky. If you have any early data, even from a small sample, make use of it. 'In our initial pilots, we saw users complete [task] 50% faster.'

Don't underestimate the power of a clearly articulated vision and a credible product roadmap. While prospects are purchasing your current solution, they are also investing in your future. If you can persuasively communicate where you are heading and how you plan to achieve that, it can build confidence, especially among early adopters who wish to align with forward-thinking partners.

As a founder, your passion for your business is one of your most potent persuasive tools. It's infectious. When you genuinely believe in what you are doing and can express that enthusiasm, it captivates people. Prospects can sense authenticity and your conviction can be far more compelling than a polished yet passionless pitch from a seasoned salesperson at a large corporation.

However, there is a fine line between infectious enthusiasm and overwhelming zeal. Your passion should energise the conversation, not dominate it. It needs to be balanced with the active listening we discussed and a clear focus on the customer's needs, not just your brilliant product. Channel your excitement into gaining a deeper understanding of their problems and into demonstrating how enthusiastic you are about the prospect of helping them succeed.

Finally, persuasive communication should always lead somewhere. Every sales interaction, whether it's an email, a call or a presentation, should conclude with a clear, confident call to action (CTA). What do you want the prospect to do next? Don't leave them guessing. Make it easy for them to take the next step.

Your CTA should be specific and low-friction. Instead of a vague 'Let's talk more sometime,' try 'Would you be open to a twenty-minute call next Tuesday or Thursday afternoon where I can show you exactly how this could work for your team?' Or, at the end of a discovery call: 'Based on what we've discussed, the logical next step seems to be a brief demo focused on X and Y. Do you have 30 minutes available early next week?'

Confidence in asking for that next step is key. If you've done a good job of listening and persuasively communicating value, then proposing a next step is a natural and helpful progression, not a pushy imposition. Remember, you're guiding them towards a solution for their problems. Mastering these persuasive communication techniques will enable you to do that with grace, authenticity and increasing success.

KEY TAKEAWAYS

- Persuasion is about clarity, credibility and connection – not pressure.

- The words you choose can open or close the door to the sale.

- Every conversation should guide the prospect toward a clear next step.

FOUNDER'S FIELDWORK

Develop a Mini-Story Library: write three short anecdotes that highlight how you've helped someone solve a real business challenge.

Message Mirror: record a short version of your pitch. Play it back and ask: Would I buy this? Is it clear? Is it compelling?

Framing Flip: rewrite one feature of your product as a benefit, then again as a value-based outcome.

CTA Audit: review your last five outreach emails. Were the calls to action clear, direct and action-oriented?

Audit Your Sales Deck: ensure each slide answers either: 'So what?' or 'What's in it for the customer?'

Eliminate Jargon: revisit your pitch or emails and rewrite one using simpler, conversational language.

Chapter nine

NEGOTIATION STRATEGIES FOR WIN-WIN OUTCOMES

'In business as in life, you don't get what you deserve, you get what you negotiate.' – Chester L. Karrass

Negotiation as Collaboration, not Combat

All right, you've navigated the early stages of the sales conversation. You've listened intently, understood their needs and persuasively communicated how your fledgling product or service can make a real difference to their B2B operation. Now comes a phase that can make even seasoned entrepreneurs a little jittery: negotiation. The mere word can conjure images of high-stakes boardroom battles, aggressive tactics and someone walking away feeling as though they've lost. But here's the good news: for you, the startup founder, negotiation doesn't have to be a fearsome beast. In fact, when approached correctly, it's just another constructive conversation, a chance to collaboratively shape a deal that benefits both you and your new customer.

Let's reframe what negotiation means in the context of founder-led B2B sales. This isn't about one-upmanship or squeezing every last drop out of the other side. It's about finding common ground, ironing out the details and ensuring that the agreement you reach is sustainable and valuable for both parties. Think of it less as a battle to be won and more as a collaborative problem-solving exercise. You're not trying to 'beat' your prospect; you're trying to build the foundation for a fruitful partnership. This shift in perspective is crucial.

For a startup, aiming for a 'win-win' outcome isn't just a feel-good platitude; it's a strategic imperative. Your first customers are incredibly precious. They aren't merely entries on a sales ledger; they are your early adopters, your sources of invaluable feedback, your future case studies and potentially your most vocal advocates. If you begin this relationship by making them feel cornered or short-changed in a negotiation, you're poisoning the well before you even take a sip. A deal that leaves both sides feeling positive, however, sets the stage for a robust, long-term relationship.

As the founder, you bring unique strengths to the negotiating table. You possess an unparalleled understanding of your product, its capabilities and its limitations. You can often be more flexible and creative than a salesperson in a larger, more bureaucratic organisation. Your passion for your solution and your direct commitment to its success can be incredibly reassuring to a potential B2B client. They aren't merely speaking to a sales rep; they're engaging with the visionary, the person who can make things happen. This is a significant advantage, so don't underestimate it.

However, being the founder also presents potential pitfalls in negotiation. Your emotional investment in your 'baby' can sometimes cloud your judgment. You might be so desperate for those first few crucial deals that you're tempted to concede too much, thereby setting unsustainable precedents. Conversely, you might be so convinced of your product's brilliance that you become inflexible. Recognising these potential biases is the first step to mitigating them. This chapter focuses on equipping you with practical strategies to navigate these waters confidently and secure outcomes that truly benefit your new venture.

Preparation is Your Superpower
The first and, arguably, most important rule of negotiation is this: the party that is best prepared usually achieves the better outcome. Preparation isn't just advisable; it's the bedrock of successful negotiation. Rushing into a negotiation without doing your homework is akin to assembling flat-pack furniture without consulting the instructions – messy, frustrating and unlikely to yield a good result. Spend quality time contemplating the upcoming discussion before you even pick up the phone or walk into the room.

Begin by clearly defining your goals. What does an ideal outcome from this negotiation look like for your startup? Be specific. Is it a certain price point, a particular contract length, specific payment terms or a commitment to a case study? Next, determine your realistic target – what you would be very pleased to achieve. And crucially, what is your walk-away point? This is your Best Alternative To a Negotiated Agreement (BATNA). What's the absolute minimum you can accept before it's better to politely decline the deal? This isn't just about the headline price; consider all aspects of the deal.

Understanding your BATNA is incredibly empowering. It provides you with the confidence to stand firm on your essential requirements because you know you have a viable alternative, even if that alternative is simply 'focus on finding a different prospect who is a better fit'. Without a clear walk-away point, you risk being pushed into a deal that could genuinely harm your business in the long run. Be brutally honest with yourself here. It's better to have no deal than a genuinely bad deal, especially in the early days.

Your preparation should also involve attempting to understand the perspectives of the other side. What are their likely goals for this negotiation? What pressures are they facing? What constraints are they under? Revisit what you learned about their Ideal Customer Profile (Chapter Five) and through your active listening (Chapter Seven). The more you can anticipate their needs and motivations, the better you can tailor your approach and pinpoint areas of potential compromise that would benefit both parties.

Additionally, try to gauge their alternatives. Are they considering other vendors? What are those vendors likely offering? Or is their main alternative simply continuing with their current inefficient process? Understanding their options allows you to assess your relative leverage. If you provide a unique solution to a pressing problem that they cannot easily resolve elsewhere, your leverage increases. Conversely, if they have many similar alternatives, you will need to exert more effort to demonstrate your superior value.

Before the negotiation begins, identify potential concessions you might be willing to make. These are your 'tradeables'. Not every point will hold equal importance to you. Perhaps you could be flexible on payment terms if they commit to a longer contract or offer a slight discount if they agree to be a public case study (which is hugely valuable for a startup). Considering these trade-offs in advance prevents you from making panicked concessions in the heat of the moment. Crucially, always strive to obtain something in return for any concession you make – it's a negotiation, not a giveaway.

Finally, practise articulating your key points, particularly those related to your value proposition and your non-negotiable terms. Role-playing the conversation with a mentor or even just discussing it aloud can help you feel more confident and prevent you from being caught off-guard by predictable questions or pushback. Nowadays, you can even use tools like ChatGPT and other large language models to simulate the negotiation. The goal isn't to memorise a script but to feel comfortable and fluent with your core arguments.

With your preparation complete let's consider some core principles for conducting the negotiation itself. The first is to maintain control of the process, not the individual. This does not mean being domineering; it means guiding the conversation, suggesting agendas, clarifying next steps and ensuring the discussion remains productive. If you initiated the sales process, it is often natural for you to take the lead in structuring the negotiation.

Active listening, as we've stressed before, remains paramount during negotiation. It is not merely about politely waiting for your turn to speak; it is about actively endeavouring to understand the underlying reasons for their requests or objections. Allow them to talk. Often, the more they speak, the more you learn about their priorities, flexibility and real bottom line. Resist the urge to interrupt or to immediately counter every point they make.

Asking great questions is a powerful negotiation tool. Instead of making assumptions, use open-ended questions to explore their position. 'Can you help me understand why that particular term is so important for you?' 'What would need to happen for this proposal to work for your team?' 'If we were able to address X, would Y then be achievable?' Questions like these encourage dialogue and can uncover hidden needs or alternative solutions.

A key negotiation principle is to focus on interests, not just stated positions. A prospect's position might be, 'We need a 20% discount on your advertised price.' That's what they say they want. Their underlying interest, however, might be, 'We have a fixed budget for this quarter and your current price is slightly over,' or 'We need to demonstrate to our management that we secured a good deal.' If you can uncover the interest, you might discover more creative ways to satisfy it than simply slashing your price. Perhaps phased payments could assist with their budget or an added-value service could justify the price.

It's also crucial to separate the people from the problem. Negotiations can sometimes become tense, particularly if the other side employs aggressive tactics. Remain professional and concentrate on the objective issues being discussed, rather than on personalities. Do not take their tactics personally. If they are being difficult, it is often a negotiating strategy and not a reflection on you or your product. Maintaining your composure is key. Whenever possible, anchor the discussion around objective criteria. This could include industry benchmarks, market rates for similar services, the clear ROI your solution will deliver (as demonstrated in your sales process) or even standards set by third parties. Saying, 'Our pricing is based on the significant value we provide, including an average X% cost reduction for clients like you,' is much stronger than simply saying, 'That's our price.'

Now, let's explore a few common negotiation tactics you might encounter from B2B buyers and how you, as a founder, can respond. One of the most frequent is the straightforward price squeeze: 'Your competitor is 10% cheaper,' or 'That's more than we budgeted for.' Your first response shouldn't necessarily be to offer a discount. Instead, calmly reiterate the unique value your solution provides (Chapter Three). You might ask, 'I understand budget is a key consideration.

Can we revisit the specific ROI we projected this solution would deliver for you?' If price remains a genuine obstacle, consider whether there are ways to adjust the scope of your offering to meet their budget, without devaluing your core product. Perhaps a slightly reduced feature set or a different service tier could work. Or, if you truly believe your price reflects fair value and you're at your walk-away point, be prepared to politely stand firm. Sometimes, demonstrating confidence in your pricing can actually increase perceived value.

Another common tactic is 'the nibble'. This occurs when you believe you've agreed on all the main points and then, just as you're about to conclude, they say, 'Oh and could you just throw in free premium support for the first year?' or 'We'll also need an extra two user licences at no charge.' These small, last-minute requests can accumulate. Your response could be, 'We can certainly discuss adding premium support. How would that fit into the package and pricing we just agreed upon?' Or 'I understand that would be valuable. Let's look at that. If we add X, we might need to adjust Y slightly to keep the overall package balanced.' The key is to not simply give it away, but to treat it as a new point for discussion or a trade-off.

You might also encounter the 'good cop/bad cop' routine, where one person on their team is very friendly and seems to love your solution, while another is aggressive, critical and raises numerous objections. The aim is to make you concede to the 'bad cop' to please the 'good cop'. The best way to handle this is to remain calm, listen to the concerns raised by the 'bad cop' and address them logically and professionally. Don't get drawn into the drama or feel pressured to make concessions simply to smooth things over.

Sometimes, prospects may use an artificial deadline or create a sense of urgency: 'We need your best and final offer by tomorrow, or we're going with another vendor.' While some deadlines are genuine, others are tactics to pressure you. Don't let yourself be rushed into making a poor decision. You can respond with, 'I understand your timeline is tight. I'll do my best to expedite things on my end while ensuring we put together a proposal that accurately meets your needs. Can you help me understand what's driving the urgency on your side?' This demonstrates willingness without committing you to an immediate, ill-considered concession.

Next is the 'appealing to a higher authority' tactic: 'This looks great, but I'll have to run it by my boss/the committee/legal.' This can sometimes serve as a way to stall or to revisit later asking for more concessions. While it is often legitimate, strive to grasp the full decision-making process and the criteria of that higher authority earlier in your sales discussions. You might ask, 'That's perfectly understandable. To help that conversation go smoothly, what are the key criteria that your boss will require for approval?'

Balancing Flexibility and Boundaries

One of the greatest advantages for you as a startup founder is the ability to negotiate beyond just the headline price. This is often where you can discover creative win-win solutions. What else can you offer that is low-cost for you but high-value for them? Alternatively, what can you request that is high-value for you but relatively easy for them to provide? Consider a value exchange.

Perhaps the most valuable non-price currency for a startup is social proof. Can you negotiate for a glowing testimonial, a detailed case study (once they've seen results) or their agreement to act as a reference customer? These assets are marketing gold and can be far more valuable in the long run than a slightly higher upfront price on a single deal. Don't hesitate to ask for these things, especially if you are making a concession elsewhere.

Payment terms can also be a point of negotiation. If a prospect is budget-constrained, offering more flexible payment terms (e.g. quarterly instead of annual upfront or a slightly delayed first payment) might assist them in signing the deal, provided it aligns with your cash flow. Conversely, you might offer a small discount for full upfront payment if that benefits your startup.

Consider the scope of work or service levels. If their budget is tight, is there a 'lite' version of your offering that you could provide? Or could you offer an enhanced service level (e.g. dedicated onboarding support, faster response times) as a value-add instead of a price cut? As the founder, you often possess the flexibility to tailor these aspects more easily than a large company.

You can also explore future business or partnership opportunities. 'If this initial project is successful, what are the potential avenues for us to expand our work together?' While this isn't a concrete concession, understanding the long-term potential can sometimes make you more willing to be flexible on an initial deal, as long as it doesn't put you at a disadvantage. A word of warning here, though: these 'jam tomorrow' offers, as they are known, rarely come to fruition unless you continue to chase and remind your clients that these were discussed initially. Your work in negotiation never stops; it's constant and part of your account management approach.

Throughout the negotiation, your mindset is key. Aim for confident humility. You need to be confident in the value you provide and the fairness of your position, but also humble enough to listen to their needs and be willing to find common ground. It's not about being a pushover, nor is it about being arrogant or inflexible. It's about being a reasonable, professional businessperson seeking a mutually beneficial agreement.

Crucially, don't be afraid to say 'no' and walk away from a deal if it's not right for your business. Sometimes, the best outcome of a negotiation is realising that an agreement isn't possible on terms which make sense for you. This is where knowing your BATNA is vital. Walking away from a bad deal frees you up to find a good one. It also signals that you value your offering and that you aren't desperate, which can paradoxically increase your negotiating power in future interactions. Many times in my life in sales, I have walked away from a prospect only for them to follow me as I am leaving and ask me to return to continue the negotiation. Try it one day when you are buying a car!

You'll inevitably encounter situations where the prospect seems to hold all the cards – perhaps they're a very large, well-known company and you're a tiny, unknown startup. In these power-imbalance situations, don't be intimidated. Focus on your unique value proposition, your niche expertise, your agility as a small company and the direct access they get to you, the founder. Often, larger companies are looking for innovative solutions from nimble startups precisely because they cannot obtain that kind of focus or cutting-edge thinking from their established, larger vendors.

Embrace a 'lean negotiation' approach. Just as with your product development, every negotiation presents a learning opportunity. After each one, whether you win or lose the deal, take a few moments to reflect. What worked well? What didn't? What tactics did they use? How did you respond? What would you do differently next time? This continuous learning will make you a more effective negotiator over time.

Once you've reached a verbal agreement on the key points, it is good practice to send a brief email summarising what was discussed and agreed upon. This helps prevent misunderstandings later and sets a clear foundation for any formal contract that follows (which we'll discuss further in Chapter Twenty). Keep it simple and factual: 'Great speaking with you. Just to confirm, we agreed on X, Y and Z, with next steps being A and B.'

Finally, always strive to conclude the negotiation on a positive and professional note, irrespective of the outcome. If you have reached an agreement, express your enthusiasm for the partnership. If you have not been able to reach a deal, thank them for their time and consideration and keep the door open for potential future collaborations. The B2B world can be smaller than you think and maintaining good relationships is always a wise strategy.

KEY TAKEAWAYS

- Great negotiations aim for mutual value, not victory.

- Preparation builds confidence and control.

- Concessions should be traded, not given away – always link a give with a get.

FOUNDER'S FIELDWORK

BATNA Builder: define your Best Alternative To a Negotiated Agreement before your next sales conversation.

Define Your Walk-Away Point: write down your non-negotiables before your next pricing or contract discussion.

Trade Matrix: list what you're willing to trade (e.g. payment terms, support levels) and what you want in return.

Prepare Three Value Levers: identify three things you can add (not discount) to sweeten a deal – e.g. onboarding help, extended support.

Role-Play a Negotiation: ask a colleague or mentor to act as a tough prospect. Practise handling price pressure calmly. Practise saying no to a discount request while preserving the relationship.

Create a Win-Win Cheat Sheet: for each deal in your pipeline, write what success looks like for both you and the customer.

Plan Your First Ask: in your next negotiation, make the first offer to set the anchor point.

Chapter ten

BUILDING RAPPORT AND TRUST WITH CLIENTS

'Trust is built on credibility and credibility comes from acting in others' interests before your own.' – Stephen M.R. Covey

Rapport before Revenue

Right, you're in the game. You've grasped your value proposition, know who you're addressing, have listened attentively and started to communicate persuasively. Excellent. However, B2B sales, particularly for a fresh-faced startup founder, aren't merely a sequence of logical arguments. At its core, it's still about human connection. This chapter focuses on two of the most vital ingredients in that connection: rapport and trust. Without them, even the most brilliant product and the most compelling pitch can fall flat. With them, you can begin to overcome the natural scepticism that B2B buyers have towards a new, unproven vendor.

Consider rapport as the initial spark, the friendly understanding that makes conversation flow effortlessly. It's about discovering common ground and creating a comfortable atmosphere. Trust, conversely, is a deeper, more solid foundation. It's the conviction that you are credible, reliable and genuinely have their best interests at heart. Rapport can secure a pleasant meeting; trust, however, is what closes the deal, especially when you're asking them to take a chance on your startup. For an entrepreneur who embodies the face, voice and oftentimes the entire sales team of their new business, deliberately and authentically building each of these is not just a valuable skill – it's your super-glue.

As a founder, you possess a hidden advantage here. While you may lack a portfolio of renowned client logos or decades of company history, you have something powerful: authenticity. Your genuine passion for the problem you're addressing and the solution you've implemented can be incredibly compelling. When you merge this with a conscious effort to forge rapport and earn trust, you begin to level the playing field. This chapter will explore practical ways to achieve just that, without feeling like you need to become a cheesy, back-slapping caricature.

First impressions, as the old saying goes, count. And in the B2B world, they count significantly, especially when you're the new kid on the block trying to get a foot in the door. From your very first interaction – be it an email, a cold call or a scheduled video meeting – you're setting the tone. Professionalism is the baseline. This means clear, error-free written communication, being on time (which entails arriving a few minutes early for calls or meetings) and being thoroughly prepared. These aren't just courtesies; they are immediate, tangible signals that you respect their time and that you are organised and reliable – these are the early seeds of trust.

But professionalism doesn't mean being a robot. You're a founder, likely driven by a unique vision. Allow a bit of that personality to show, appropriately. If you're on a video call, your virtual handshake matters. Make an effort with your appearance – you don't need a three-piece suit (unless that's the norm in their industry) but looking presentable demonstrates that you take the interaction seriously. Ensure your background is uncluttered and professional. Test your tech beforehand. These small details remove friction and help your message, along with your genuine desire to connect, to come through more clearly.

Building genuine rapport is about establishing a human connection beyond the purely transactional. It's about making the other person feel comfortable and understood. One of the simplest ways to start is by doing a little light, non-intrusive research before you speak. A quick scan of their LinkedIn profile might reveal a shared alma mater, a common interest or a mutual connection. Perhaps their company was recently in the news for a positive achievement. A brief, sincere mention of something like this can be an excellent icebreaker and show you've taken an interest in them beyond just a potential sale. 'I saw your company just won the X award – congratulations, that's quite an achievement!'

Using someone's name correctly and naturally throughout a conversation is another small but significant rapport builder. It shows respect and acknowledges them as an individual. While you don't want to be a blatant copycat, subtly mirroring the other person's pace and tone can sometimes help create a sense of alignment. If they speak slowly and deliberately, you might moderate your own naturally fast pace. If they are more formal, you might dial back your casualness a notch. The key here is subtlety; it should feel natural, not as though you're mimicking them. Don't be afraid to use appropriate humour if the moment feels right and aligns with your personality. A shared chuckle can instantly warm up a conversation. However, tread carefully here – what's funny to one person might not be to another, especially across different cultures or industries. When in doubt, keep it light and err on the side of professional congeniality.

Above all, genuine rapport comes from showing a sincere interest in them and their business. Your active listening skills are paramount here. Ask questions about their challenges, their goals and their industry. When people feel that you are truly interested in their world, not just in making your pitch, rapport naturally follows.

Small Signals, Big Impact

While rapport is the oil that lubricates the conversation, trust is the engine that drives the relationship forward. In a B2B sales context, trust isn't some vague, fuzzy feeling. It's a prospect's concrete belief in several key things about you and your startup: your competence (that you know what you're doing and your solution works), your integrity (that you're honest and will do what you say) and your benevolence (that you genuinely care about their success and aren't just trying to make a quick buck). As a new venture, you're starting with a trust deficit. They don't know you. Your product is unproven in their eyes. Their natural inclination is scepticism, a defence mechanism against perceived risk. Your job is to patiently and consistently lay the bricks of trust.

Let's borrow and adapt a well-known concept, often called the 'Trust Equation', to the startup sales scenario. Think of Trust as being built from Credibility + Reliability + Connection (or Intimacy), all divided by the prospect's Perception of Risk. As a founder, you need to actively work on increasing the upper elements while reducing that denominator.

Credibility involves demonstrating that you know your stuff. This stems from a deep understanding of your product, your industry and, critically, the specific challenges your prospect faces. When you can speak intelligently about their world and confidently explain how your solution fits, your credibility score improves. Don't be afraid to admit what you don't know. Bluffing or fabricating information is a surefire way to destroy trust if you're caught out (and you usually are). Honesty, even if it means saying 'That's a great question, let me find out the definitive answer and get back to you,' builds far more credibility in the long run. Sharing relevant insights or helpful information, even if it's not directly tied to your product, also positions you as a knowledgeable resource, not merely a salesperson. And remember, your founder story, your expertise, the very reason you started this company – these are powerful credibility builders.

Reliability is perhaps the most straightforward component of trust to build, yet it's where many fall short. It boils down to one simple principle: do what you say you will do. If you promise to send a follow-up email by the end of the day, send it. If you schedule a call for 2 pm, be ready by 1.55 pm. If you say your product can do X, ensure it can. Every small commitment you meet reinforces the perception that you are dependable. For a startup with an evolving product, setting realistic expectations is doubly important. It's always better to under-promise and over-deliver, especially in these early days. Be transparent about your product's current capabilities. If a feature is on the roadmap but not yet live, say so. Honesty about limitations, coupled with a clear plan to address them, is far more trustworthy than trying to sell vapourware.

Connection, or what some call intimacy in the Trust Equation, is about the human element, demonstrating that you care about their success. This is where your active listening and genuine empathy shine. When you consistently focus the conversation on their needs, their goals and how you can help them achieve what they want, you signal that this isn't just about you. Offer advice or assistance if you can, even if it doesn't lead directly to an immediate sale. Perhaps you know someone who could help them with an unrelated problem, or you've read an article that's highly relevant to a challenge they mentioned. Being genuinely invested in helping them solve their problems, whether your product is the full answer or just part of it, fosters a sense of partnership and builds that crucial 'benevolence' aspect of trust. Here, something which may be counterintuitive to you is very important. If you don't succeed in making a deal the first time and you feel they are an ideal client, keep building on this connection. Continue to offer help, email them articles you think may assist them and check in with them every few months; it will have a significant impact on your future dealings.

Transparency is the clear water in which trust grows and it is especially critical when you are a new, unknown entity. Be upfront about your company's stage. You don't need to proclaim 'We're a tiny startup!' from the rooftops in a way that undermines confidence, but attempting to present yourself as a massive, established corporation when you are not is a recipe for trouble. Instead, frame your startup nature as a strength: 'As a focused, founder-led company, we're incredibly agile and responsive to our early clients' needs.' Be clear about your pricing, your terms and your processes. If your product has limitations or if certain features are still in development, be open about it, but also enthusiastic about your roadmap and your commitment to improvement. Prospects can handle the truth; they cannot handle feeling deceived. Many in fact enjoy being involved in the development of your business and offering and will give you their time freely to help you, even if they are not yet a customer.

Now, let us specifically address the 'newness' factor. How do you build trust when you lack a long list of impressive client logos or years of glowing testimonials? You lean into the unique advantages of working with a founder-led startup. Emphasise the direct access they have to you, the decision-maker, the visionary. Highlight your ability to be nimble and adapt to their needs in a way that larger, more bureaucratic competitors cannot. Share your passion and your long-term vision for the company and the solution – this can be very reassuring. 'We're in this for the long haul and our early partners are incredibly important to us; their success is our success.' But this does not mean that you build and do everything they suggest. You must be mindful of creating a product or service that has the broadest appeal at this stage. This is a mistake which software startups often make, ending up with multiple versions that become hard to maintain. Honesty is the key to this discussion with prospects.

Consider offering ways to reduce their perceived risk. Pilot programmes, proof-of-concept projects, or even extended trial periods (if suitable for your product) can enable them to experience your value firsthand before making a significant commitment. If you have any early feedback from beta testers or initial users, even if it is informal (and you have their permission to share it), leverage it. A positive quote or a brief story about how you have already assisted someone can start to build that crucial third-party validation.

In today's predominantly virtual sales environment, cultivating trust and rapport digitally requires conscious effort. Your online presence, however simple, must be professional. A clean, informative LinkedIn profile for you as the founder is essential. If you possess a company website, even a basic one-pager, ensure it is clear, error-free and effectively conveys your core message. Your email etiquette also plays a role. Are your emails clear, concise and professional in tone? Do they offer value?

Video calls are now a staple of B2B sales. Make the most of them to foster connection. Good lighting (so they can see your face clearly), a decent camera and microphone, and minimising distractions all contribute to a more professional and engaging experience. When you are speaking, look at the camera as much as possible – it is the virtual equivalent of eye contact. Use these visual cues to convey your attentiveness and enthusiasm. Even something as simple as remembering details from previous conversations and referencing them shows you are paying attention and that they are more than just another call on your calendar.

Consistency, Follow-Through and Credibility

Building rapport and trust isn't a one-time task you simply tick off a list. It's an ongoing process that must be nurtured throughout the entire sales cycle, from the initial cold email to the final handshake (or virtual equivalent). Every touchpoint is an opportunity to reinforce or, unfortunately, erode that foundation. Consistency is your ally. If you're responsive and helpful during the initial discovery phase, but then slow and dismissive once they seem interested, you'll ruin any trust you've built.

Addressing their initial questions and concerns with empathy and transparency is crucial. Consider these not as roadblocks but rather as opportunities to build more trust. If they raise a concern about your product's maturity, don't become defensive. Acknowledge their perspective 'That's a perfectly valid question, especially when considering a newer solution like ours') and then address it honestly, perhaps by highlighting your rigorous testing process, your experienced development team or your commitment to rapid iteration based on early client feedback.

At times, demonstrating a touch of appropriate vulnerability can actually strengthen trust. This doesn't mean appearing incompetent or unsure. It means being human. If they pose a particularly tough question, for which you don't have an immediate, polished answer, it's perfectly acceptable to say something like, 'That's a really insightful question and, to be perfectly transparent, it's something we're actively working on refining. Our current approach is X and our commitment to clients like you is Y. We value that kind of input as it helps us build a better solution.' This kind of honesty is often far more reassuring than a glib or evasive answer.

Remember, B2B buyers, particularly those contemplating a new vendor, seek partners they can depend on. They want to feel assured that you'll support them, that you comprehend their business and that you're devoted to their success. By intentionally concentrating on cultivating genuine rapport from the initial interaction and then methodically constructing credibility, reliability, connection and transparency, you, as the founder, can convert scepticism into belief and prospects into your first pivotal clients.

KEY TAKEAWAYS

- Trust is built in small moments – by showing up, listening and delivering.

- Rapport accelerates the sales process by reducing perceived risk.

- Consistency and transparency are more powerful than charisma.

FOUNDER'S FIELDWORK

Trust Builders List: identify five small behaviours you can commit to consistently (e.g. punctuality, honest timelines).

Send a Warm Follow-Up: after your next meeting, send a message that mentions something personal or specific they shared.

Use the 'three x three Rule' Before Calls: spend three minutes finding three personal or company facts about your prospect (LinkedIn, blog, press).

Customer Insight Check-in: start your next sales call with, 'Last time you mentioned X – is that still a priority?' Track how that deepens rapport.

Build a Relationship Timeline: for your top three leads, list three ways to add value in the next thirty days without pitching.

Introduce a Warm Intro: ask a mutual contact to introduce you to a prospect, then pay it forward by offering an intro of your own.

Create a Rapport Journal: after each call, jot down small personal details (hobbies, family, style) to reference later.

Chapter eleven

HANDLING OBJECTIONS WITH GRACE AND EXPERTISE

'Objections are not rejections; they are simply requests for more information.' – Bo Bennett

Welcoming Objections, not Dodging Them

So, the conversation is flowing, you're hitting your stride and then it comes: the objection. That moment when your B2B prospect raises a concern, a doubt or an outright reason why they might not want to proceed. For many entrepreneurs, especially when you're new to sales and deeply passionate about your product, an objection can feel like a slammed door, a personal critique or, at the very least, a major roadblock. But here's a vital reframe: objections aren't necessarily bad news. In fact, they are often a sign of engagement. A prospect who raises an objection is usually thinking, considering and trying to understand if your offering truly fits their needs. Silence or polite, non-committal nods can be far more worrying.

As a startup founder, you can expect to encounter your fair share of objections, possibly more than an established company. Your business is new, your product might still be evolving, your brand isn't yet a household name (even in its niche) and B2B buyers are inherently risk averse. They're looking for reasons not to choose you because doing so often feels safer. Your job isn't to argue them out of their objections, but to handle them with grace, empathy and expertise, turning potential deal-breakers into opportunities to clarify value and build even deeper trust. This chapter is your guide to doing just that, using your unique position as the founder to your advantage.

Your first and most crucial reaction to an objection sets the tone. If you become defensive, flustered or dismissive, you've already damaged the conversation. Remember that deep well of confidence and resilience we talked about in Chapter Two? Now's the time to draw from it. Your prospect isn't attacking you personally, even if it feels like they're questioning your 'baby'. They are expressing a legitimate concern from their perspective. Your goal is to meet that concern with understanding and helpful information. Stay calm. Breathe. And then, listen. Really listen. Often, the objection you hear first isn't the real objection or at least not the complete story. It might be a symptom of a deeper concern, a polite way of expressing a different issue or simply a request for more information.

Before you jump in with a brilliant rebuttal, ensure you fully understand what they are truly asking or worrying about. This is where your active listening skills, honed in Chapter Seven, become absolutely critical. Do not interrupt. Allow them to articulate their point fully. Sometimes, simply giving them the space to talk might lead them to answer their own objection or clarify it in a manner that makes it easier to address.

The Real Issue behind the Question
A practical and highly effective framework for handling objections, especially suited to the consultative approach that a founder should adopt, is the LAER model: Listen, Acknowledge, Explore, Respond. Let us break down how that would function for an entrepreneur.

Listen: we have covered this but it bears repeating. Give your prospect your undivided attention. Hear the words but also endeavour to understand the emotion or underlying concern behind them. Are they worried? Sceptical? Confused? This active listening provides the crucial data you require for the next steps.

Acknowledge: this is where you validate their feelings or concerns without necessarily agreeing with the substance of the objection. Simple phrases like, 'I understand why you'd ask that', or 'That's a perfectly fair point' or 'I can see why that might be a concern for you', can work wonders. This immediately lowers their defences. You're not fighting them; you're showing that you've heard them and respect their perspective. This builds rapport (Chapter Ten) and makes them more receptive to what you say next. For instance, if they say, 'You're a new company; how do we know you'll be around in a year?' a good acknowledging response would be, 'That's a very reasonable question to ask when considering partnering with a newer business like ours.'

Explore: this is arguably the most crucial step and it's where many salespeople fall short. Before you offer a solution or a counter-argument, dig deeper. Ask clarifying questions to ensure you understand the root of their objection. 'Could you tell me a bit more about what specifically concerns you regarding our company's age?' or 'When you say the price is higher than you expected, what were you comparing it to, or what budget did you have in mind for solving this particular problem?' For a startup, exploring is vital because the objection might be based on a misunderstanding of your innovative product, your lean business model or the specific value you offer to a niche like theirs. Perhaps they assume your newness means a lack of expertise when, in fact, your founding team has decades of relevant experience. You won't know unless you explore.

Respond: only once you have truly listened, acknowledged their right to the concern and explored the underlying reasons do you offer your response. And this response shouldn't be a generic, canned answer; it should be tailored to the specific nuances you've uncovered. This is where your deep product knowledge, your understanding of your Unique Value Proposition (Chapter Three), your compelling narrative (Chapter Four) and your persuasive communication skills (Chapter Eight) all come together. Your response should aim to alleviate their specific concern by providing relevant information, offering a different perspective or demonstrating how your solution, despite their initial objection, is indeed the right fit for them.

Now, let's delve into the trenches and examine some of the common objections B2B entrepreneurs are likely to encounter and how the LAER model can be applied.

1. Price and Budget Objections: these are probably the most frequent. 'It's too expensive.' 'We don't have the budget for this right now.' 'Your competitor, BigEstablishedCorp, offers a similar thing for less.'

Listen: hear them out. Don't immediately leap to defend your price.

Acknowledge: 'I understand that budget is a key consideration for any business, especially when evaluating new solutions.'

Explore: 'To help me understand better, when you say it's too expensive, are you comparing it to another specific solution or is it primarily about fitting it into your current budget allocation for this area? Or 'Could you share a bit about how you're currently valuing a solution to the problem of [reiterate the pain point their business is facing]?'

Respond: this is where you pivot back to value. 'While our upfront price might seem higher than some alternatives, our clients typically find that the X% reduction in [specific cost] or the Y% increase in [specific revenue driver] means our solution actually delivers a significant return on investment within Z months. For example...' (Use your UVP and any early data or projections). If it's a genuine budget constraint, you might explore options such as phased implementation, different service tiers or adjusted payment terms, as discussed in negotiation (Chapter Nine). For the competitor comparison, highlight your differentiators: 'Yes, BigEstablishedCorp has a different price point, but they often serve a much broader market. We focus specifically on businesses like yours, which means [mention a unique benefit relevant to them, like faster onboarding, more tailored features, or direct founder access for support].'

2. Product, Feature, or 'Maturity' Objections:
'Your product doesn't have X feature.' 'Is your platform stable and scalable enough for our needs?' 'This looks interesting, but it feels a bit... new.'

Listen: let them voice their concerns about specific functionalities or the perceived risks of a newer product.

Acknowledge: 'That's a valid question about feature X and it's important that any solution you choose meets your core requirements.' Or 'I understand why you'd want to be sure about the platform's maturity and scalability.'

Explore: 'Could you tell me more about how you envision using feature X and what problem it would solve for you?' (People buy outcomes, not necessarily that exact feature, and you might have another way to achieve it.) 'What are your specific concerns regarding scalability or stability based on what you've seen or your past experiences?'

Respond: be honest about your current capabilities. If you don't have a feature, don't pretend you do. You could say, 'Feature X isn't in our current release, though it's something we're actively evaluating for our roadmap based on feedback from early partners like yourselves. However, many of our clients find they can achieve a similar outcome for [problem X solves] by using our Y and Z features in this way...' For maturity concerns, talk about your development process, your team's expertise, any beta testing you've done or your commitment to support. Frame your startup agility: 'One of the advantages of working with a focused company like ours at this stage is that we can be incredibly responsive to the needs and feedback of our early clients, often incorporating improvements much faster than larger, more established vendors.'

3. 'Newness', Credibility and Risk Objections:
'You're a startup; how do we know you'll still be in business next year?' 'We typically partner with established vendors.' 'We've never heard of your company before.'

Listen: these are very real fears for B2B buyers. Don't dismiss them.

Acknowledge: 'That's a perfectly understandable concern when considering a newer company. You need assurance that your partners are stable and reliable.'

Explore: 'What has been your experience in the past with newer vendors, or what are the key things that would give you confidence in a company at our stage?'

Respond: this is where your founder story and passion can truly shine. Talk about your vision, your funding (if applicable and appropriate), your team's commitment and any early traction or milestones. 'While we are a newer name in the market, our founding team has X years of experience in this industry and we started this company because we saw a critical gap that existing solutions didn't address. We are deeply committed to our clients' success because it's fundamental to our own.' You could also discuss any risk-mitigation measures you offer, such as pilot programmes, phased rollouts, strong service level agreements (if you have them) or even an escrow arrangement for source code if that's relevant for your type of business and the client's scale. Highlight the benefits of being an early adopter: 'Our early partners get unparalleled access to our team and a genuine opportunity to help shape the future direction of a product that's being built to solve their exact problems.'

4. 'Status Quo' or Inertia Objections:
'We're reasonably happy with our current solution/process.' 'It seems like too much effort to switch right now.' 'This isn't a top priority for us at the moment.'

Listen: this is often the most significant competitor for an innovative startup – the gravitational pull of 'the way things have always been done.'

Acknowledge: 'I understand. It's natural to stick with what's familiar and change always requires some effort.'

Explore: this is where you gently challenge their assumptions about how 'happy' they truly are. 'You mentioned you're reasonably happy but earlier you noted that [reiterate a pain point they mentioned]. How much is that particular issue costing you in terms of time or resources each month?' Or 'If you could wave a magic wand and improve one aspect of your current process for [relevant area], what would it be?' For the 'not a priority' objection: 'I appreciate that you have many competing priorities. Could you share what some of your top initiatives are for this quarter? Sometimes, improving [the area your product addresses] can actually help accelerate those other goals.'

Respond: focus on the clear, quantifiable cost of not changing versus the benefits of adopting your solution. Make the transition seem as painless as possible. 'We've designed our onboarding process to be incredibly straightforward, and many of our clients are surprised at how quickly they can get up and running. We'd handle much of the heavy lifting. The real question might be, what's the ongoing cost of not addressing [the core problem] for another six months?'

5. 'I Need to Think About It' or Stall Objections: this is often a polite smokescreen for an unvoiced objection.

Listen: patiently.

Acknowledge: 'Of course, it's important to give this proper consideration.'

Explore: gently try to uncover the real issue. 'I understand. When you say you need to think about it, what are the specific aspects or questions that are top of mind for you as you weigh this decision?' Or 'To ensure I've provided all the information you need, are there any particular areas of concern or anything that's still unclear?'

Respond: based on what they reveal, address that underlying concern. If they genuinely just need time, propose a clear and specific next step with a timeline. 'Perhaps it would be helpful if I summarised the key benefits we discussed in an email and we could schedule a brief fifteen-minute follow-up call for next Tuesday to see if you have any further questions then?' This keeps the momentum going and makes it harder for the deal to simply fade away.

Responding, not Reacting

Once you've listened, acknowledged and explored, you'll need to respond. Here are a few proven techniques, particularly useful for startups:

The 'Feel, Felt, Found' Method: this is excellent for addressing emotional or experience-based objections. 'I understand how you feel about [their concern]. Many of our early clients felt the same way when they were first considering a newer solution like ours. However, what they found once they started working with us was that [positive outcome/benefit that directly counters their concern].' This demonstrates empathy and provides a relatable example.

Reframe/Re-label the Objection: sometimes, you can turn a perceived negative into a positive. If they say, 'You're a very small team,' you could respond, 'That's true and it means that, as our client, you get direct access to the key decision-makers, including myself as the founder. We're incredibly focused and can offer a level of personalised attention that larger companies often struggle to provide.'

The Conditional Close (or 'If... then'): this helps you test if an objection is the only thing holding them back. 'I appreciate your concern about [the objection]. If we were able to, say, offer a phased implementation to address that concern about initial workload, then would you be comfortable moving forward with the proposal?' If they say yes, you know that's the key issue to resolve. If they hesitate or raise another objection, you know there's more to uncover.

The Boomerang Technique: skilfully redirect the objection back to the prospect as a reason to buy. Prospect: 'We're worried about the time it will take our team to learn a new system.' You: 'That's a very common concern and it's precisely why we've invested so much in making our platform incredibly intuitive and our onboarding process very streamlined. Our goal is to get your team comfortable and seeing value within days, not weeks, so you can quickly overcome the time sinks in your current methods.'

Pre-empting Common Objections: as you gain experience, you will start to anticipate common objections, particularly those related to being a startup. Do not wait for the prospect to raise them. Integrate the answers proactively into your sales presentation or narrative (Chapter Four).

For example, early in your pitch, you might say, 'As a focused, founder-led company, we pride ourselves on our agility and the close partnerships we build with our early clients, ensuring they get exactly what they need.' This addresses the potential 'you're too new/small' concern before it even surfaces.

What happens if, after all your skilful listening and responding, the objection is genuinely valid and your product, at least in its current state, simply isn't a fit for their specific, critical need? This is where professionalism and long-term thinking come into play. Don't try to force it. It's far better to gracefully acknowledge the mismatch than to sell them something that will ultimately lead to their dissatisfaction and damage your young company's reputation.

You could say something like, 'Thank you for clarifying that. Based on your critical need for X feature right now, I can see that our current offering might not be the perfect fit for you at this precise moment. We are, however, planning to incorporate functionality like that in our Q4 release. Would it make sense for us to briefly reconnect then to see if the timing is better?' This shows integrity, respects their needs and keeps the door open for the future. Remember, the B2B world is often smaller than you think and, leaving a positive impression, even without a sale, is always a good strategy.

Finally, every objection you encounter, whether you overcome it or not, is a priceless piece of market intelligence for your startup. Don't let these insights evaporate. Keep a simple log or note of the objections you hear most frequently. Discuss them with your co-founder or team (if you have one). What patterns are emerging? Do these objections highlight a weakness in your product that needs to be addressed?

Is your value proposition unclear on a certain point? Do you need to refine your Ideal Customer Profile to target businesses where these objections are less likely to arise?

Utilise this feedback loop to iterate and improve. Your ability to learn from objections and adapt your product, messaging and sales approach is a hallmark of a successful lean startup. Handling objections isn't merely about saving a single deal; it's about building a more resilient product and a more effective sales process for all future deals. Approach each one with grace, listen with expertise and witness those roadblocks transform into stepping stones.

KEY TAKEAWAYS

- Objections are part of progress, not a sign of failure.

- Listen fully before responding – the real concern is rarely the first thing said.

- Address objections with curiosity and confidence, not defensiveness.

FOUNDER'S FIELDWORK

List Your Top Five Objections: write out the most common objections you hear (e.g. 'too expensive') and your ideal responses.

Use the Objection Reframing Formula: Objection   Empathy   Clarify   Respond   Confirm. Practise with each of your top objections.

Build a Live Objection Log: after every sales call this week, record any objections and how you handled them. Look for patterns.

Role-play an Objection Round: ask a peer or mentor to play a 'difficult' prospect. Practise staying calm and curious.

Develop a 'No Hard Feelings' Response: craft one graceful message to send when a deal is lost – it can still build goodwill for future contact.

Chapter twelve

NAVIGATING DIFFICULT CONVERSATIONS AND CHALLENGING CLIENTS

'The quality of your life is the quality of your conversations.' – Susan Scott

When Tension Rises, Stay Rooted

Let's be frank: no matter how brilliant your product, how smooth your sales pitch or how delightful your personality you will inevitably encounter difficult conversations and, yes, challenging clients. It's as certain in the world of B2B sales as coffee and early mornings. For you, the entrepreneur pouring your heart and soul into a new venture, these situations can feel particularly tough. It's easy to take them personally or view them as a sign that you're doing something wrong. But here's the reality: these moments are not failures; they are tests. They assess your professionalism, problem-solving skills, resilience and your ability to turn a tricky situation into a manageable, or even positive, outcome. This chapter aims to equip you to face these inevitable bumps in the road, not with dread but with a clear head and a practical toolkit.

Consider your early B2B clients as your first dance partners. Some will be graceful and intuitive, following your lead and making the whole experience a joy. Others might have two left feet, tread on your toes or insist on doing the Macarena when you're trying to waltz. Your job isn't to storm off the dance floor but to find a way to either get back in rhythm or, in rare cases, politely seek a new partner. As the founder, you are uniquely positioned to handle these sensitive interactions. You possess the deepest understanding of your offering and the authority to make decisions that can resolve issues swiftly.

Difficult conversations in a startup sales context can take many forms. Perhaps a client's expectations haven't quite matched the reality of your evolving product. Maybe there's a misunderstanding concerning the scope of work you agreed to. Payment discussions can sometimes become uncomfortable. Or you might simply have a client whose communication style is, shall we say, abrasive. Then there are clients who, despite your best efforts, seem perpetually dissatisfied or make demands that stretch your lean startup resources to breaking point. Recognising the type of challenge you're facing is the first step to addressing it effectively.

Before you engage in any difficult conversation, the most crucial step is to prepare your mindset. Your emotional state will significantly influence the tone and outcome. It's natural to feel frustrated, anxious or even angry, especially if you believe your startup is being unfairly criticised or taken advantage of. However, entering a conversation filled with negative emotions is akin to pouring petrol on a smouldering ember. Take a moment (or several) to cool down. Remind yourself that your goal is to find a constructive solution, not to 'win' an argument or prove the client wrong.

Professionalism is your armour. Maintain a calm, respectful demeanour, even if the other party does not. Remember all that effort spent on building resilience from Chapter Two? This is where it truly pays off. Try to detach your personal feelings from the business issue at hand. The client's frustration is likely directed at the situation, not at you as an individual, even if it doesn't always sound that way.

Preparation also involves gathering the facts. Before you address an issue, ensure you have a clear understanding of the situation from your perspective. Review the initial agreement or contract. Look back at relevant email correspondence. Understand the history of the relationship. What exactly was promised? What has been delivered? Where did the wires get crossed? Entering a difficult conversation armed with clear facts, rather than vague recollections, places you on much firmer ground.

Consider your desired outcome. What might a reasonable resolution look like for both you and the client? What are you willing to concede and where do you need to stand firm? Understanding your own boundaries and objectives in advance helps you navigate the conversation more effectively and prevents you from making hasty decisions under pressure.

Lastly, think about the timing and medium for the conversation. A quick, reactive email sent during an emotionally charged moment can often escalate a problem. For sensitive issues, a phone call or a video meeting is typically far more effective, as it allows for better nuance and a more human connection. Select a time when you can dedicate your full attention to the conversation, free from distractions.

As the conversation begins, your active listening skills (remember Chapter Seven?) are your most valuable asset. Allow the client to express their grievances fully without interruption, even if you disagree with every statement. Your primary role is to comprehend their perspective, no matter how distorted it may seem to you. Use those acknowledging phrases: 'I understand you're frustrated about X,' or 'I can see why Y is a concern for you.' This doesn't imply you concur with their assessment, but it does indicate you acknowledge their feelings, which is crucial for de-escalation.

Once they've had their say and you've genuinely listened, it's time to calmly and clearly state your perspective, sticking to the facts as you understand them. Use 'I' statements rather than accusatory 'you' statements. For example, instead of saying, 'You constantly change the requirements,' try, 'I understand the project has evolved and my understanding of our initial agreement was for X, Y and Z. The additional requests for A, B and C seem to fall outside that original scope.' This focuses on the issue and your perception of it, rather than blaming the client. The goal is to shift the dynamic from confrontation to collaboration. Frame the issue as a shared problem that you both want to solve. 'Okay, it sounds like there's a disconnect between what you were expecting regarding feature X and what our current version delivers. How can we work together to bridge that gap or find a workaround that meets your immediate needs?' By inviting them into the problem-solving process, you empower them and increase the chances of finding a mutually acceptable solution.

Throughout the conversation, maintain transparency. If your startup made a mistake, own up to it quickly and sincerely. 'You're absolutely right, we dropped the ball on delivering that report by Tuesday. I apologise for that oversight and here's what we're doing to rectify it and ensure it doesn't happen again.' A genuine apology, coupled with corrective action, can often defuse a tense situation and even strengthen trust. People understand that new businesses, in particular, are learning and evolving. Honesty is usually appreciated far more than excuses. In fact, you may see the problem before the customer does. If this is the case, put the resolution in place, then ring the customer, own up to the mistake and explain the resolution you have put in place, including the method you are using to ensure a similar issue does not arise in the future. As a buyer, when I had these conversations with my suppliers, they always resulted in a much closer relationship. Remember that.

Setting Boundaries with Clarity and Compassion
Now, let's consider some common types of challenging clients and specific strategies for navigating those relationships.

The Scope Creeper: this client is notorious for the 'Oh, and just one more little thing...' syndrome. Those 'little things' can quickly accumulate, derailing your timelines and eroding your profitability, which is especially perilous for a lean startup.

Strategy: from the outset, ensure your initial agreement or contract clearly defines the scope of work. When a new request arises that feels like scope creep, gently but firmly refer back to that agreement. 'That's an interesting idea. Based on our initial agreement which covered X and Y, this new request for Z would be outside that scope. I'm happy to put together a separate proposal for Z if you'd like to explore it as an additional piece of work.' Having a process for changing orders, even if it's a simple email confirmation of the new scope and any associated costs, is crucial. It's not about being difficult; it's about valuing your time and ensuring you're compensated for the work you do.

The Unhappy Client (Product/Service Not Meeting Expectations): despite your best efforts, a client might feel your offering isn't delivering what they anticipated.

Strategy: first, investigate thoroughly. Is it a genuine product flaw? A misunderstanding of how a feature works? Or were their initial expectations unrealistic, perhaps due to a miscommunication during the sales process? Apologise for their frustration. If there's a genuine issue on your end, be transparent about it and explain how you'll address it (a bug fix, a workaround). If it's a misunderstanding, patiently re-educate them. Sometimes, simply spending extra time helping them use the product effectively can resolve their dissatisfaction. Consider offering a partial refund, a discount on future services or some other goodwill gesture if appropriate, especially for an early client whose long-term satisfaction is vital. Every piece of negative feedback, while painful, is a gift that can help you improve your product or your communication.

The Late/Non-Payer: cash flow is king for any startup and clients who don't pay on time can be a major source of stress.

Strategy: have clear payment terms in your agreement from day one. Send polite, automated reminders as invoices become due. If an invoice becomes overdue, a friendly follow-up call is often more effective than increasingly stern emails. Try to understand their situation – sometimes it's a genuine oversight or a temporary cash flow issue on their end. 'Hi [Client Name], just following up on invoice #123. Is everything okay on your end?' If they are facing difficulties, you might consider offering a short-term payment plan. However, you also need to be firm. You're running a business, not a charity. If non-payment persists despite your efforts, you may need to pause services (as per your contractual rights) or, in extreme cases, consider options for debt recovery, though hopefully, it rarely gets to that point for a B2B client.

The Overly Demanding Client: some clients appear to believe that, because they're paying you, they own your every waking moment. They may have unrealistic expectations regarding response times, demand endless revisions or generally consume a disproportionate amount of your limited startup resources.

Strategy: setting clear boundaries early in the relationship is crucial. Define your standard response times for support or queries in your service agreement. For revision requests, refer back to what was agreed upon. Occasionally, a frank but respectful conversation is needed: 'We value your business immensely and we're committed to providing excellent service. To ensure we can do that effectively for all our clients, including yourselves, we need to work within the agreed-upon communication channels and project parameters.' Learn to say 'no' politely when requests are truly unreasonable. 'Unfortunately, providing 24/7 on-demand support isn't something we can offer with our current service package, but we will always respond within X hours during business days.'

The Client Who 'Ghosts' You: you've had good interactions, perhaps even started a project, and then suddenly... silence. Emails go unanswered, calls go to voicemail.

Strategy: don't assume the worst immediately. People get busy and emails get buried. Try various methods of re-engagement over a week or two – a polite follow-up email, a brief voicemail. You could try a subject line like 'Following up on X project – just checking in.' If there's still no response, send one final polite message stating that you assume they are currently occupied but you're available if they wish to reconnect. Then, for your own sanity and resource planning, mentally move on. You can't force engagement.

In all these scenarios, your role as the founder presents both a burden and an advantage. The burden is that the buck stops with you; you can't easily escalate it to a 'manager'. The advantage is that clients often respect the direct involvement of the founder. You can make decisions and offer solutions on the spot that might be more difficult for a regular employee. Use this authority wisely. Your willingness to personally step in to resolve an issue can be a powerful demonstration of your commitment.

It's also important to recognise the emotional toll these situations can take on you as an entrepreneur. Constantly dealing with negativity or conflict is draining. Ensure you have support systems in place, whether it's a co-founder, a mentor or simply a friend to whom you can vent. Refer back to the resilience-building techniques from Chapter Two. Taking breaks and maintaining perspective are crucial for your own well-being.

Turning Conflict into Constructive Dialogue

Often, a difficult conversation, if handled well, can actually strengthen a client relationship. When a client sees that you are willing to listen, acknowledge problems and work constructively to find solutions, it can build a deeper level of trust than if everything had gone perfectly smoothly. They recognise that you are a reliable partner, even when challenges arise. Moreover, these challenging interactions provide invaluable learning opportunities. They can highlight weaknesses in your processes, ambiguities in your contracts, areas where your product requires improvement or warning signs to watch for when qualifying future prospects.

There will, however, be rare occasions when a client relationship is simply unsalvageable or is so detrimental to your startup's resources, morale or reputation that the best course of action is to part ways. 'Firing' a client is a very difficult decision for any business and especially for a startup desperate for revenue. However, sometimes the cost of retaining a truly toxic or chronically unprofitable client is far higher than the revenue they contribute. If you have exhausted all reasonable attempts to resolve issues, if the client consistently acts in bad faith, makes unreasonable demands that undermine your team or is abusive, it might be time to consider ending the relationship.

If you reach this point, handle it with extreme professionalism. Consult any contractual obligations regarding termination. Communicate your decision clearly, calmly and in writing, stating the reasons briefly and factually, without assigning blame. 'After careful consideration of our ongoing working relationship and the challenges we've faced in aligning on X and Y, we've come to the difficult decision that we are no longer the best fit to provide services for your company. We will, of course, honour our commitments through [date] and do everything we can to ensure a smooth transition.' Offer to assist them in transitioning to another provider if feasible. Your goal is to disengage as cleanly as possible and minimise any potential negative fallout.

Navigating difficult conversations and challenging clients is an acquired skill. You won't always get it right, especially in the early days. However, by approaching these situations with preparation, empathy, a focus on problem-solving and a commitment to professionalism, you'll not only survive them but also become a stronger, more resilient entrepreneur, thereby building a more robust business in the process.

KEY TAKEAWAYS

- Difficult conversations are inevitable – and often lead to breakthroughs.

- Boundaries are a sign of strength, not avoidance.

- With the right mindset and language, conflict can create trust

FOUNDER'S FIELDWORK

Write a Difficult Message Draft: pick a real (or likely) scenario – missed deadline, unhappy client – and draft a candid, empathetic message.

Create a Conversation Prep Template: include What's the issue? What outcome do I want? What does the client probably feel? What's my ask?

Use the 'XYZ' Model: for giving feedback. 'When you do X, I feel Y, because Z.' Practise this in a non-sales situation.

Define Your Boundaries: write down three red flags or deal-breakers for customer behaviour you won't tolerate (e.g. disrespect, scope creep).

Schedule a 'Temperature Check' Call: with one client or prospect, ask directly how they feel about working with you so far.

Post-Conversation Debrief: after a difficult client call, reflect. What went well? What could improve? What triggered me?

Chapter thirteen

LEAD GENERATION: BUILDING A PIPELINE OF QUALIFIED PROSPECTS

'You can't sell anything to someone who doesn't know you exist.' – Lori Richardson

Why a Full Pipeline Fuels Confidence

All right, so you've got your mindset tuned, your confidence building, your value proposition starting to sing and you know who you're trying to reach. Fantastic. But all that foundational work is like having a beautifully designed fishing rod and a perfectly crafted lure... with no fish in the pond. This chapter is about stocking that pond. We're diving into the detail of lead generation – the art and science of attracting potential B2B customers who might actually want to buy what you, the intrepid entrepreneur, are selling. For a startup, this isn't just a marketing activity; it's the very lifeblood that fuels your early sales efforts and, ultimately, your survival and growth.

Let's be clear from the outset: lead generation for a founder just starting up looks very different from how a big, established corporation with a dedicated marketing department and a hefty budget does it. You don't have a massive brand presence drawing people in. You don't have a legion of salespeople dialling for dollars. What you do have is ingenuity, a deep understanding of the problem you solve (because you probably lived it) and the ability to be nimble and try things that bigger players might overlook. This chapter is about leveraging those founder superpowers to build a pipeline of qualified prospects without breaking the bank or your spirit.

First, what exactly is a 'lead' in the world of your B2B startup? Simply put, it's an individual or a business that has shown some level of interest in your product or service or that fits your Ideal Customer Profile (ICP) so well that they should be interested. A 'qualified prospect' takes it a step further – it's a lead that you've vetted to some degree and determined possesses a genuine potential need, the capacity to buy (even if budget discussions are down the line) and aligns with the type of customer you can successfully serve. Your goal isn't just to collect a random list of names; it's to build a predictable, albeit initially small, flow of these qualified opportunities. This is what we mean by building a pipeline.

Before you even think about specific tactics, remember that your Ideal Customer Profile (Chapter Five) is your North Star for lead generation. Every activity you undertake to find potential customers should be aimed squarely at attracting or identifying businesses and individuals who fit that profile. Trying to generate leads from 'everyone' is a recipe for wasted effort and a pipeline full of duds. Your compelling Value Proposition Narrative (Chapter Four) is the bait on your hook – it's what will attract them once you find them.

The entrepreneurial journey of lead generation is a marathon, not a sprint. You're not going to open the floodgates overnight. Consistency is far more important than occasional heroic bursts of activity. It's about steadily building momentum, learning what works and iterating. This 'lean sales approach' we've discussed applies perfectly here. Try a few things, see what sparks a flicker of interest, do more of that and discard what doesn't. Resourcefulness is your best friend. You'll be surprised at what you can achieve with a bit of cleverness and a lot of hustle.

Focus on Fit, not Just Volume

At its core, effective B2B lead generation for a startup revolves around a few fundamental principles. First, targeting is everything. We cannot stress this enough. Know your ICP inside out and focus your efforts exclusively on reaching them. Second, lead with value. In a world saturated with sales pitches, offering genuine assistance, insight, or a solution to a small part of their problem before you ask for anything in return is a powerful way to cut through the noise and build initial trust. Third, while a multi-channel approach is beneficial eventually, do not spread yourself too thin initially. Choose one to three channels that seem most promising for reaching your ICP and concentrate on mastering those before introducing more complexity. Fourth, even basic tracking and measurement are crucial. You need to know where your leads are originating and which activities are actually yielding results, however modest. Finally, never forget to leverage your unique founder superpowers: your unshakeable passion, your deep product knowledge and the direct access you can offer.

To even begin capturing leads, you need a few foundational elements in place. Do not worry, this does not mean a fancy, expensive website on day one. Your 'home base' can be a very simple one-page website or a well-crafted landing page. What's essential is that it clearly articulates your UVP, explains who you help and what problem you solve and has an obvious way for interested parties to get in touch or learn more. Think clarity, credibility and a clear call to action.

You will also need some basic lead capture mechanisms. This could be a straightforward contact form on your landing page, your direct email address clearly displayed or a means for people to sign up for a future newsletter or product update (even if that newsletter is just you sending occasional valuable insights for now).

And, as we have mentioned, your professional online presence, primarily a polished and complete LinkedIn profile, is non-negotiable. It is often the first place a B2B prospect will look to check you out.

Now, let's discuss some broad strategies for generating leads. The subsequent chapters will delve deeper into the 'how-to' of prospecting, social selling, content marketing, cold outreach and networking, but this chapter focuses on understanding how they fit into the overall picture of building that initial pipeline.

One of the most immediate and often overlooked goldmines is leveraging your existing network. These are your 'warmest' potential leads or sources of referrals. Consider past colleagues, university friends, mentors and individuals you've met at industry events (even virtual ones), as well as friends and family who might know people in your target market. The key is to approach them thoughtfully. Don't just spam your entire contact list with a generic sales pitch. Instead, personalise your outreach. Explain what you're doing, who you're trying to help and ask if they know anyone facing the specific challenges your solution addresses. A warm introduction from a mutual connection is incredibly powerful. Remember to always offer to return the favour.

Next, there is the concept of direct outreach. This involves proactively identifying companies and individuals who fit your ICP and reaching out to them directly. Chapter Seventeen, 'Cold Outreach: Making it Work for You,' will delve into the mechanics of doing this effectively but the core idea is to research potential prospects and initiate contact with a tailored message that highlights how you might be able to help them. It requires persistence and a thick skin but it's often a necessary component of early-stage B2B lead generation.

Content as a magnet is another powerful approach, though it's more of a medium-to-long-term strategy. As Chapter Sixteen, 'Content Marketing for Lead Nurturing', will explore, creating valuable, relevant and consistent content (like blog posts, short articles, insightful LinkedIn posts or even simple checklists) that addresses the pain points of your ICP can attract them to you. Instead of hunting them down, they find you because you're offering expertise. Even sharing curated content from other sources, along with your own insightful commentary, can help position you as a useful resource.

Social selling, particularly through platforms like LinkedIn, will be covered in detail in Chapter Fifteen. For now, recognise that this involves more than just having a profile. It's about actively engaging with your network, sharing valuable insights, participating in relevant group discussions and connecting with potential prospects in a non-salesy manner, building relationships that can later turn into sales opportunities.

Networking, both online and offline (when feasible), remains a potent source of leads. Chapter Eighteen will address 'Networking and Building Strategic Partnerships'. Every conversation you have is a potential opportunity to learn, connect or find a lead. Consider industry-specific online forums, LinkedIn groups, virtual meetups or even local business groups. Your goal isn't to pitch to everyone you meet but to build genuine connections and remain alert for opportunities where you can offer assistance.

Designing a Repeatable System

Once you begin generating these initial trickles of interest, you absolutely cannot afford to let them slip through the cracks. This is where even a simple lead management process becomes essential. You don't need a complex, expensive Customer Relationship Management (CRM) system from day one but you do need something. As per the book's requirement to focus on free or low-cost tools, consider the following:

A dedicated spreadsheet (Google Sheets, Excel): this is the simplest starting point. Create columns for contact name, company, email, phone, lead source (how did you find them?), date of first contact, notes from your interactions and the next action step.

Trello or Asana: these project management tools can be adapted for basic sales pipeline tracking. Each lead can be a 'card' that you move through stages like 'New Lead', 'Contacted', 'Follow-up Scheduled', 'Demo Done', etc.

Free CRM Tiers: many established CRM providers (like HubSpot, Zoho, Freshsales) offer free versions that are more than adequate for a solo founder. These provide more structure than a spreadsheet and can help you manage contacts, track interactions and even send emails. Investing a few hours to learn a free CRM can save you a lot of headaches down the line.

What should you minimally track for each lead?

Contact Information: full name, job title, company, email, phone number, LinkedIn profile, URL.

Lead Source: where did this lead originate? (e.g. network referral, LinkedIn outreach, website contact form.) This helps you understand which lead generation activities are effective.

Key Pain Points/Needs: what problems are they attempting to solve? (Learned from your initial interactions.)

Interaction History: dates and brief notes from calls, emails and meetings.

Next Action & Date: what's the next step with this lead and when will you take it? This is crucial for follow-up.

Lead Status: (e.g. New, Contacted, Qualifying, Demo Scheduled, Proposal Sent, Closed-Won, Closed-Lost). As leads start arriving, you must swiftly distinguish the wheat from the chaff. This is lead qualification, which becomes even more critical when your time and resources are exceedingly limited. You cannot afford to spend valuable hours pursuing leads that are unlikely to convert or that do not suit your startup.

While established companies may utilise complex scoring systems, you can begin with a simpler approach. Consider these key questions for each lead:

1. ICP Fit: how closely do they align with your Ideal Customer Profile? Are they in the appropriate industry, the right size and experiencing the problems you resolve?

2. Recognised Pain: do they possess a genuine pain point that your solution directly addresses? More importantly, do they acknowledge it as a pain they wish to resolve?

3. Engagement/Interest Level: how responsive have they been? Did they proactively reach out, or did you initiate contact? Do they appear genuinely interested?

4. Realistic Expectations (for a startup): do they seem receptive to collaborating with a newer company? Do they comprehend that your product, while addressing their core problem, may still be developing?

5. Decision-Making Ability (or influence): are you conversing with someone who can genuinely make or significantly influence a purchasing decision? (While this follows the classic BANT – Budget, Authority, Need, Timeline – for a startup, Authority and Need are often the initial barriers. Budget and Timeline may be more adaptable or become clearer as you demonstrate value.)

A 'hot' lead for you might be a company that perfectly matches your ICP, has explicitly stated it is struggling with the exact problem your solution fixes and is eager to learn more. A 'cold' lead might be someone who vaguely fits your ICP but has not shown any real engagement. Prioritise your follow-up efforts on the hotter leads.

As the founder, you are the chief lead generator in these early days. This is not a task you can easily outsource when you're just starting and still refining your messaging and understanding your market. Embrace this role.

Every conversation you have and every email you send in an attempt to generate a lead is a direct feedback mechanism. You will learn what resonates, what falls flat, what questions people ask and what their real pains are. This intelligence is invaluable for iterating on your product, your UVP and your ICP.

Do not get discouraged if the initial volume of leads is low. It almost certainly will be. Early B2B lead generation often prioritises quality over quantity. A handful of genuinely qualified prospects with whom you can build real relationships are far more valuable than hundreds of unqualified names on a list. Set realistic expectations for yourself. Your goal is to create a small but steady trickle of opportunities that you can then nurture through your sales process.

The leads you generate through these efforts are the raw material for the prospecting strategies we will discuss in the next chapter. Prospecting is the more focused activity of actively pursuing these qualified leads to turn them into concrete sales opportunities. Lead generation fills the top of your sales funnel; prospecting moves them down it.

Remember, building a pipeline is an ongoing process. It is about consistently planting seeds. Some will sprout quickly, others will take time and some will not sprout at all. Your job as the entrepreneurial salesperson is to keep planting, keep nurturing and keep learning which soil and which seeds yield the best harvest. The efforts you put into lead generation today are what will sustain your sales efforts tomorrow and lay the groundwork for your startup's future success.

KEY TAKEAWAYS

- A healthy pipeline reduces pressure on every deal and boosts sales confidence.

- Focused, qualified leads outperform mass-market lists.

- Systematic prospecting ensures consistency, not just activity spikes.

FOUNDER'S FIELDWORK

Pipeline Forecast Worksheet: define your revenue goal, average deal size and conversion rate. Reverse-engineer how many leads you need each month.

Create a Simple Lead Tracker: use a spreadsheet or CRM to list twenty potential leads. Include name, contact method, status and notes.

Set a Weekly Prospecting Goal: choose a manageable number (e.g. ten new contacts/week) and block out time to reach them.

Map Your Lead Sources: identify three high-potential places your ideal customers hang out online (e.g. forums, Slack groups, LinkedIn).

Design a Lead Magnet: create one simple asset – e.g. a checklist, cheat sheet or short guide – that would attract your ideal customer.

Track Response Rates: send ten outreach messages and record open rates, replies and conversions. Optimise accordingly.

ICP Alignment Review: audit your last 10 leads – how many were a strong match to your Ideal Customer Profile?

Lead Source Scorecard: track where your best leads came from in the past 60 days. Invest more in those channels.

Chapter fourteen

PROSPECTING STRATEGIES FOR THE MODERN B2B LANDSCAPE

'Prospecting – find the man with the problem.' – Ben Friedman

Intentional, not Interruption-Based

You've laid the groundwork: you understand what a lead is, you've begun to build a pipeline (however small) as we discussed in Chapter Thirteen and you have your Ideal Customer Profile firmly in mind. Now what?

Leads sitting in a spreadsheet or a basic CRM are like unplanted seeds; they have potential, but they won't grow into revenue-generating clients on their own. This is where prospecting comes into play. Prospecting involves the proactive, often gritty work of engaging those leads, qualifying them further and transforming them into genuine sales opportunities. For you, the startup founder juggling a dozen other critical tasks, mastering a few smart prospecting strategies for the modern B2B landscape isn't just important – it's how you'll turn those initial sparks of interest into the conversations that will build your business.

Think of lead generation as casting a wide net to see who swims into it. Prospecting is like carefully examining each fish you've caught, deciding which ones are the keepers and then figuring out the best way to, well, get them interested in what you're offering. It's a focused, often personalised effort. In today's B2B world, this means being smarter, more targeted and more value-driven than ever before. Gone are the days of blindly sending out thousands of generic emails or making hundreds of uninformed cold calls, hoping something sticks. The modern prospector is a researcher, a problem-solver and a strategic communicator, all rolled into one. As a founder, your inherent understanding of the problem you solve gives you a unique edge in this pursuit.

Your mindset going into prospecting is critical. This isn't about being a pushy salesperson trying to hit a quota; it's about genuinely trying to find businesses you can help. Adopt the mindset of a consultant or a helpful expert. Your primary aim in the initial stages of prospecting isn't to close a deal but to initiate a meaningful conversation and determine if there's a mutual fit. This requires patience, persistence (because you will face silence and rejection) and a commitment to providing value at every touchpoint. Remember, especially as a startup, that you're building relationships, not just chasing transactions.

With a pipeline of leads from Chapter Thirteen, your first prospecting task is to prioritise. Not all leads are created equal and, as a founder with limited time, you need to focus your energy where it's most likely to yield results. Revisit your Ideal Customer Profile (ICP) from Chapter Five. How closely does each lead match this profile? You can create a simple tiering system. 'Tier A' leads might be a perfect ICP match, perhaps from a company that has shown previous interest or is in an industry you know you can serve exceptionally well. 'Tier B' leads might be a good fit but may require a bit more research to confirm the pain point. 'Tier C' leads might be more speculative. Start by focusing your most intensive prospecting efforts on your Tier A leads.

Beyond just ICP fit, look for 'trigger events'. These are occurrences within a prospect's company or industry that might signal an opportune time to reach out. Has a target company recently received funding? Hired a new executive in a key role (who might be open to new solutions)? Announced an expansion or a new strategic initiative? Launched a new product that might need complementary services? Tools like Google Alerts, industry news sites or even closely following target companies on LinkedIn can help you spot these triggers. Referencing a relevant trigger event in your outreach shows you've done your homework and makes your approach timely and relevant. For example, 'I saw your company recently announced X initiative, which often creates challenges around Y – our solution helps businesses like yours navigate exactly that.'

Modern Tools, Timeless Principles

Thorough research is the backbone of any effective modern prospecting strategy. Before you even consider crafting that first email or picking up the phone, you need to understand who you're communicating with. This isn't about stalking; it's about professional due diligence that enables you to personalise your approach and demonstrate genuine interest. Start with the company. What do they actually do? Who are their customers? What are their stated goals or mission? What challenges are they likely facing based on their industry, size or recent news? Their website (particularly the 'About Us', 'Careers' and 'Blog/News' sections) is a good starting point. Then, investigate the specific individual you intend to contact. What is their role and what are their responsibilities? What does their LinkedIn profile reveal about their career path, their skills or any content they've shared or commented on? Do you have any mutual connections? The aim is to uncover a piece of information that can help you build rapport or tailor your message. Perhaps they wrote an article you found insightful or their company recently published a case study that resonates with the problem your startup solves. The more specific and relevant your initial point of contact, the greater your chances of cutting through the noise.

With your research completed, you need a strategy for how you'll attempt to engage your prospects. This is often referred to as a prospecting cadence or sequence – a series of touchpoints across different channels (email, LinkedIn, perhaps phone) over a defined period. A single email or call is rarely sufficient to elicit a response from a busy B2B professional. The modern approach involves multiple, value-added interactions.

For a startup founder, this does not need to be overly complex. A simple cadence might look like this:

Day 1: Personalised email referencing your research and offering a specific point of value or a relevant insight.

Day 3: LinkedIn connection request (with a brief, personalised note referencing your email or a common interest).

Day 5 or 6: Follow-up email, perhaps offering a different piece of valuable content (such as a short article, a relevant statistic, or a brief case study if you have one, even an anecdotal one from early use).

Day 9 or 10: A final, polite follow-up email, or if you're comfortable and it's appropriate for your target audience, a phone call.

The key to a successful cadence is that each touchpoint should feel like a natural continuation, not a random barrage or some computer-generated sophisticated 'spam'. The key phrase here is personalised. Each message should offer a slightly different angle or piece of value and always be respectful of their time. Avoid simply resending the same email with 'Just checking in' – that adds no value. Personalisation is paramount. Generic sequences get ignored. Your research should inform every step. This multi-touch approach significantly increases your chances of being noticed at the right time, as B2B priorities can shift quickly.

When crafting that initial outreach message, whether it's an email or a LinkedIn InMail, remember the WIIFM principle: 'What's In It For Me (the prospect)?' Your message must be laser-focused on them, their potential problems and how you might be able to help. Keep it concise – no one has time to read a novel from an unknown sender. Clearly state who you are and why you're reaching out, referencing the specific piece of research that made you think they'd be interested. Avoid jargon and overly salesy language. Your call to action should be clear and low-commitment. Instead of asking for a sixty-minute demo, aim for a brief 15–20-minute exploratory call to discuss their challenges and see if there's a potential fit. As the founder, your outreach carries unique weight. You can convey a level of passion and deep understanding that a generic sales rep often can't.

Don't forget the power of warm introductions. We touched on leveraging your network in the previous chapter on lead generation. When it comes to prospecting, an introduction from a mutual connection is like getting a VIP pass to the front of the queue. It dramatically increases your chances of receiving a response and starting a positive conversation. When asking for an introduction, make it incredibly easy for the person facilitating the connection.

Provide them with a brief, forwardable blurb about who you are, what you do, why you think the prospect would be interested and what your ask is (e.g. 'a brief introductory chat'). Always express your gratitude and offer to return the favour. Actively look for mutual connections on LinkedIn with your target prospects – you might be surprised by who you know in common.

Persistence with Relevance

As you engage in these prospecting activities, it is essential to have a way to manage your efforts. The basic spreadsheet or free CRM you set up for lead management in Chapter Thirteen now serves as your prospecting command centre. For each prospect, track when you reached out, which channel you used, what message you sent, any responses received and what your next planned action is. This level of organisation is vital; it prevents promising prospects from slipping through the cracks and stops you from accidentally contacting the same person multiple times with the same message (a sure route to appearing unprofessional). Setting daily or weekly activity goals for yourself – like 'research five new prospects' or 'send ten personalised outreach emails' – can help maintain consistency and momentum.

Now, what occurs when you actually get a response, or, as is often the case, when you don't? If a prospect responds positively and agrees to a conversation, fantastic! Confirm the details, conduct a little more targeted preparation for the call and get ready to apply your active listening and persuasive communication skills. If they respond with a polite 'not interested right now', thank them for their time and, if appropriate, ask if you may keep them in mind for the future or send them occasional (truly valuable) updates. Sometimes 'not now' genuinely means 'not now' and they might be a good prospect down the line.

If you receive no response after a few attempts in your cadence, do not take it personally. B2B professionals are incredibly busy. Your message might have arrived at an inconvenient time, become buried in their inbox or simply not been compelling enough for them at that moment. After a respectful number of follow-ups (your cadence should define this – perhaps 3–5 touches over a few weeks), it is usually best to move on and focus your energy elsewhere. You can always add them to a list for a much later, different type of re-engagement, perhaps if you have significant new product news or a highly relevant case study in the future. The skill is in knowing when persistent follow-up becomes pestering; people dislike being pestered by strangers!

A crucial part of modern prospecting is the willingness to iterate and improve. Not every outreach strategy or message will be a winner. Treat your prospecting efforts as small experiments. If you send out twenty personalised emails with one type of subject line or value proposition and receive a very low response rate, try a different approach with the next batch.

Perhaps your call to action is too demanding or your initial value proposition isn't hitting the mark for that segment. This is where the 'lean startup' mentality directly applies to your sales activities. Track what you're doing, measure the results (even if it's just a simple tally of responses) and be prepared to adapt.

As a founder, you're uniquely positioned to make these adjustments quickly. You don't have to wait for approval from a marketing department. You can hear feedback from a prospect in the morning and adjust your outreach message in the afternoon. This agility is a significant advantage.

Don't be afraid to try unconventional (but always professional and ethical) approaches if you think they might resonate with your specific ICP. Prospecting in the modern B2B landscape is a blend of art and science; the science lies in the research, the structured cadences and the tracking of your efforts. The art is in the personalisation, the crafting of compelling messages, the ability to build rapport quickly and the judgement to know when to push gently and when to pull back. It requires a different skill set than simply presenting to an already interested party. It's about creating that interest, often from a cold start. The strategies you employ will evolve as your company grows, as your product matures and as you learn more about what truly motivates your ideal customers. However, the foundational principles of targeted, value-driven and persistent outreach will always remain the bedrock of a healthy sales pipeline.

KEY TAKEAWAYS

- Prospecting is about discovery, not just outreach – be curious, not pushy.

- Customised, insight-led messaging outperforms generic sequences.

- Consistent effort across channels builds visibility and trust.

FOUNDER'S FIELDWORK

Choose Your Channel Focus: pick one core outbound channel to master this month (LinkedIn, cold email, event networking, etc.).

Build a 'First Touch' Script: create a templated opening message or call intro that's personalised and problem-focused.

Cadence Builder: create a 5–7 step outreach sequence combining email, LinkedIn and calls. Test and refine.

Identify Five Triggers for Outreach: list company or role changes, funding news, hiring sprees, tech stack upgrades or content shares.

Run a Five-Day Prospecting Sprint: reach out to five new leads daily for five days. Record your learnings on who responds and why.

Chapter fifteen

LEVERAGING SOCIAL SELLING FOR MAXIMUM IMPACT

'You can't automate authenticity.' – Jill Rowley

Why Social Selling Works

All right, you're now equipped with prospecting strategies and hopefully have a few initial leads or at least well-researched targets. However, in today's digitally interconnected B2B landscape, simply sending an email or making a call might not be enough to cut through the noise. This is where social selling comes into its own. If prospecting is about actively seeking out opportunities, social selling focuses on leveraging social media platforms to build relationships, establish credibility and subtly guide potential customers towards your solution. For you, the startup founder, having to be resourceful and build a personal brand alongside your company brand, mastering social selling isn't just a trendy option; it's a highly effective, low-cost way to punch above your weight and connect directly with your Ideal Customer Profile (ICP).

Let's clarify what social selling isn't. It's not about blasting your sales pitch across every social media channel. It's not about collecting thousands of superficial connections. And it's definitely not about automating impersonal messages hoping for a random bite. At its core, social selling is about using social media to find the right prospects, build rapport, understand their needs and then, when the time is right, position your offering as a valuable solution. It's a more nuanced, relationship-driven approach that aligns perfectly with the consultative selling style that benefits startups. Think of yourself as a helpful guide in their online world, not an uninvited billboard.

Why is this so crucial for an entrepreneur just starting up? Firstly, it's incredibly cost-effective. Most powerful social selling activities can be done using the free versions of platforms, primarily LinkedIn. Secondly, it allows you, the founder, to engage directly with potential customers, leveraging your unique passion and deep understanding of the problem you solve. You can build your personal credibility even before your company has a massive brand reputation. Thirdly, B2B buyers are already using social media for their own research. They're looking for insights, checking out potential vendors and seeing who's who in their industry. Being actively and thoughtfully present where your prospects are looking is simply smart business.

The mindset you bring to social selling is paramount. Approach it with a genuine desire to help and provide value. Your goal isn't to make a sale with every interaction; it's to build trust, establish yourself as a knowledgeable resource and create connections that might lead to sales conversations down the line. It's a longer game than a direct sales pitch but the relationships built are often stronger and more loyal. This is about connection over mere collection of contacts.

Choosing your digital playground wisely is the first step. While there are countless social media platforms, for B2B sales – especially for a startup founder – one platform reigns supreme: LinkedIn. It is, without a doubt, the professional network. This is where your ICP is most likely to be active in a business context, looking for solutions, connecting with peers and sharing industry insights. While platforms like Twitter (or X) can be useful for certain industries (like tech, media or for engaging with specific thought leaders) and niche industry forums can be valuable for highly targeted engagement (something we'll touch on more in networking), your primary social selling focus as a B2B entrepreneur should almost certainly be LinkedIn. For now, let's concentrate on mastering this powerhouse.

Your LinkedIn profile isn't just an online CV; it's your digital storefront, your personal landing page. When a prospect hears about you or your startup, one of the first things they'll often do is look you up on LinkedIn. What they find needs to be compelling and client-centric.

Your headline is prime real estate. Don't just put 'Founder at [Your Startup Name]'. Think about your UVP. Who do you help and what problem do you solve? Something like 'Founder at [Startup Name] | Helping B2B SaaS Companies Reduce Churn with [Your Unique Approach]' is far more informative and engaging.

Your summary or 'About' section is your opportunity to share your story and articulate your mission. This isn't merely a dry list of skills. Weave in your founder's narrative (Chapter Four). Why did you establish this company? What are you passionate about achieving for your clients? Use keywords that your ICP might search for when seeking solutions or expertise in your field.

A professional profile picture (a clear, friendly headshot) and a relevant banner image (perhaps something that represents your industry, your solution's benefit or your company branding, if you have it) are essential. They immediately convey professionalism and credibility. While you may be an avid Tottenham Hotspur supporter, a picture of you standing in their stadium on a tour is not an ideal choice for your banner image. Save that for Facebook.

Your experience section should do more than simply list past roles. For your current position as founder, highlight what your company does and the value it provides. For previous relevant roles, focus on achievements that demonstrate your expertise in the problem domain you now address.

Recommendations and endorsements serve as social proof. As a new founder, you might not have a lengthy list of client recommendations yet. Don't hesitate to ask satisfied early users, beta testers, mentors or even former colleagues (who can vouch for your skills and character) for a recommendation on LinkedIn. Offer to write one for them in return. Endorsements for relevant skills also add credence.

LinkedIn's Featured section is an excellent place to showcase your most valuable content – perhaps a link to your startup's website, a key blog post that you've written, an insightful article or a video explaining your offering.

Once your profile is optimised to attract and inform your ICP, the next step is strategic networking. This approach isn't about indiscriminately sending connection requests to everyone you come across. Quality trumps quantity. Use LinkedIn's search filters (even the free ones are powerful) to locate individuals who fit your ICP. Search by job title, industry, location and keywords. If your budget can stretch to LinkedIn Sales Navigator at some point, its advanced search and lead-building features are incredibly helpful, but you can achieve a great deal without it initially.

When you find a promising prospect, always personalise your connection request. The generic 'I'd like to connect with you on LinkedIn' is a significantly missed opportunity. A short, personalised note dramatically increases your acceptance rate and starts the relationship on a much warmer footing. Refer to something specific: 'Hi [Prospect Name], I came across your profile and was impressed by your work in [their industry/a recent project]. As a fellow [your profession/interest] focused on helping companies like yours with [briefly mention problem you solve], I'd value connecting.' Or, if you have a mutual connection or belong to a shared group, mention that.

Show, Don't Just Sell
Once connected, the goal isn't to immediately pitch. Let me reiterate, it is not to pitch. It's to engage. Pay attention to what your new connections are posting. Thoughtful comments on their updates or articles (going beyond a simple 'great post!') can be very effective. Ask a relevant question, share a complementary perspective or add a piece of valuable information. This positions you as an engaged and knowledgeable peer, not merely another silent connection.

Joining relevant LinkedIn Groups where your ICP congregates is another excellent strategy. These groups are often focused on specific industries, roles or challenges. Don't just join and lurk; listen to the discussions. What questions are people asking? What problems are they airing? When appropriate, contribute thoughtfully to the conversations. Offer helpful advice, share relevant insights (without overtly selling) and establish yourself as a valuable member of that community. This is a fantastic way to identify prospects who are actively seeking solutions.

This brings us to the role of content in social selling. While Chapter Sixteen will delve deeply into 'Content Marketing for Lead Nurturing', the sharing and engagement aspect of content is integral to social selling. You don't need to be a prolific content creator from day one. Curating valuable third-party content can be just as effective for a time-strapped founder. Find insightful articles, industry reports or relevant news pieces that would genuinely interest your ICP and share them, with your own brief commentary. Explain why you believe it's valuable or pose a question to spark discussion. This demonstrates you're staying informed and are a source of helpful information.

When you create your own content (even if it's just a short text post on LinkedIn sharing a tip or an observation), ensure it focuses on addressing your ICP's pain points or aspirations. Are you helping them solve a problem, learn something new or see an issue from a different perspective? Consistency is more important than sheer volume. A few high-value posts each week are better than daily spam. Experiment with different formats. While text posts are simple, LinkedIn articles offer more depth. Short videos (if you're comfortable creating them – even simple ones from your phone) can be incredibly engaging and help humanise you as the founder.

Now, how do you transition from these softer engagement activities to actual sales conversations? This is the 'selling' part of social selling and it requires tact and good timing. One key aspect is social listening. Pay close attention to what your prospects and connections are saying online. Are they asking questions that your product or service can answer? Are they expressing frustration with a problem you solve? These are potential buying signals. For instance, if someone in a LinkedIn group posts, 'Does anyone know a good tool for streamlining X process?' and your startup offers exactly that, you have a perfect, natural opening.

When you sense an opportunity or when you've built a degree of rapport through engagement, consider taking the conversation private via a direct message (DM) or LinkedIn InMail (if you have a premium account). Your outreach message here needs to be highly personalised. Reference your previous interactions or a specific piece of their content you found interesting. Clearly and concisely explain why you're reaching out and how you think you might be able to help them specifically. Focus on their potential needs, not just your product's features.

Your call to action should be low-friction. Instead of asking for a lengthy demo, suggest a brief exploratory chat. For example: 'Hi [Prospect Name], I really enjoyed your recent post on [topic]. It ties in closely with some of the challenges we help [their type of company] address around [specific problem]. We've developed a [your solution] that's showing great results in [specific benefit]. Would you be open to a quick fifteen-minute call next week to see if this might be relevant for your team?'

As a startup founder you don't require a suite of expensive social selling tools to get started. Your primary tool is LinkedIn itself, used thoughtfully. The free version offers robust search, profile optimisation and engagement features. If and when your budget allows, LinkedIn Sales Navigator provides much more advanced search filters, lead recommendations and insights that can significantly boost your efficiency. For scheduling content shares (if you're curating a lot), free tiers of tools like Hootsuite or Buffer can be helpful but manual, authentic engagement is often more powerful initially. Most importantly, ensure your social selling activities are somehow logged or integrated with that simple CRM or spreadsheet you're using to track leads, so you have a holistic view of your interactions with each prospect.

Measuring the impact of your social selling efforts can feel less direct than tracking email open rates, but it remains important. Here are some simple metrics you can monitor:

Profile Views: are more people (especially those fitting your ICP) looking at your optimised profile?

Connection Request Acceptance Rate: a useful measure of how well your personalised requests resonate.

Engagement on Your Posts: likes, comments and shares signify that your content is hitting the mark. Track not just the quantity but also the quality of engagement – are key prospects interacting?

Meaningful Conversations Started: how many DMs or private messages lead to actual dialogue?

Leads/Meetings Generated: ultimately, how many discovery calls or demos can you directly attribute to your social selling activities?

Do not discount the qualitative benefits either. Social selling aids in building your personal brand as a founder, establishing credibility in your niche and gaining invaluable insights into your market and the evolving needs of your prospects. Although these aspects are harder to quantify, they remain critical for long-term success.

Consistency, Community and Connection

Finally, let's highlight a few common pitfalls for entrepreneurs to avoid in their social selling endeavours. The most egregious is pushing for a hard sell too soon. Connecting with someone on LinkedIn and immediately bombarding them with a generic sales pitch is the quickest way to get ignored or even blocked. I block many people for this very approach and I also warn my connections about them. Remember, relationship first.

Inconsistent activity is another common mistake. Being extremely active for a week and then disappearing for a month sends a poor signal. Aim for sustainable, regular engagement. Ignoring interaction on your own posts or messages is also a definite no-no. If someone takes the time to comment or ask a question, respond in a timely and considerate manner.

Avoid being overly self-promotional. A good rule of thumb is the 80/20 principle: 80% of your content and engagement should focus on providing value to others, with only about 20% being directly about your company or product.

While automation tools are available, be very cautious about automating too much or inauthentically. Personalised, human interaction is your strength as a founder. Generic automated DMs are transparent and off-putting. Additionally, this approach is far less effective if you lack a clear strategy or ICP focus. Understanding who you're trying to reach and what you want to achieve will guide all your social selling actions.

Leveraging social selling for maximum impact involves playing the long game, building genuine connections and consistently providing value. As a founder, your authenticity and direct involvement are your greatest assets on these platforms. Use them wisely and you'll discover that social media can be an extraordinarily powerful engine for building your pipeline and growing your startup. Ideally, you want to be seen as a 'Knowledge Leader'; social media is one of the channels you will need to master to achieve this status in the eyes of your prospects.

KEY TAKEAWAYS

- Social selling is a visibility and credibility game – be present, be helpful.

- Thoughtful content sparks inbound interest from prospects.

- Real conversations, not broadcasts, drive results.

FOUNDER'S FIELDWORK

Optimise Your LinkedIn Profile: update your headline, summary and banner to clearly state who you help and how.

Post Three Pieces of Value Content: share lessons, frameworks or founder experiences that speak directly to your target audience.

Engage Daily on LinkedIn: leave three thoughtful comments per day on posts by your prospects or relevant industry voices.

Send Five Value-First Connection Requests: personalise each request with reference to the person's role, content or pain point.

Track Engagement Metrics: review which types of posts or messages get the most views, likes and replies – and adjust accordingly.

Content Plan: draft three short posts: one insight, one client win (anonymous), one challenge you've faced and solved.

Chapter sixteen

CONTENT MARKETING FOR LEAD NURTURING

'Content builds relationships. Relationships build trust. Trust drives revenue.' – Andrew Davis

From Stranger to Buyer

So, you've started to fill your pipeline. Through networking, initial outreach and perhaps some savvy social selling, you've identified individuals and businesses that fit your Ideal Customer Profile and have exhibited at least a flicker of interest. These are your leads – the raw material for future sales. But here's a crucial truth in B2B sales, especially for a new entrepreneur: very few of those leads will be ready to buy from you immediately. They might be aware of a problem you solve, but they may not fully grasp its impact, the various ways to tackle it or why your fledgling startup is the one to assist them. This is where lead nurturing, powered by smart content marketing, comes into play.

Consider lead nurturing as the ongoing conversation you have with prospects who aren't yet sales-ready. It's the process of building a relationship, deepening their understanding of their problem and potential solutions (including yours) and gently guiding them through their buying journey until they are prepared for a more direct sales conversation. And for a founder trying to gain traction without a hefty marketing budget, content marketing is your most potent tool for achieving this. It's about providing consistent, relevant value that keeps you top-of-mind and positions you as a trusted expert, not merely another vendor clamouring for attention.

This chapter isn't about launching a massive, multi-channel content empire that necessitates a dedicated team and a six-figure budget. That's not the startup reality. Instead, we're focusing on a 'lean content' approach to lead nurturing – practical, founder-led strategies you can implement today to engage your existing leads, build trust and move them closer to becoming paying customers, all while respecting your limited resources. Your goal is to be helpful and insightful, not just noisy.

Before you create a single piece of content, you need to understand two things: your nurturing goals and your audience's journey. What do you want your nurtured leads to ultimately do? Is it to request a personalised demo? To agree to a deeper strategic discussion about their challenges? To see your startup as the go-to authority in your specific niche? Having clear objectives will help you focus your content efforts.

Equally important is understanding where your leads are in their buying journey. Not everyone who downloads a free checklist or connects with you on LinkedIn is at the same stage of awareness or readiness. Broadly, B2B buyers move through phases like Awareness (they recognise they have a problem), Consideration (they're researching solutions) and Decision (they're choosing a vendor). While initial lead generation might capture people in the Awareness stage, lead nurturing often focuses on those in the Consideration and early Decision stages. Your content needs to meet them where they are.

Revisit your Ideal Customer Profile (ICP) from Chapter Five. What are their specific questions, concerns and information needs now that they're aware of a problem and starting to explore solutions? What jargon do they use? What keeps them awake at night? The more deeply you understand their world after they've become a lead, the more targeted and effective your nurturing content will be.

So, what type of content genuinely works for nurturing, especially when you're a founder juggling multiple roles and cannot afford weeks to produce a single polished masterpiece?

The key is to concentrate on high-value, practical content that doesn't necessarily demand Hollywood-level production. Educational content is paramount in lead nurturing. Your prospects are seeking answers and insights. You can deliver these through:

In-depth blog posts or articles: these can be hosted on a straightforward blog on your website or even published as LinkedIn Articles. They provide the opportunity to delve into a specific pain point in more detail than a quick social media update, discuss industry trends relevant to your ICP, or offer actionable advice.

How-to guides, checklists, or templates: these are extraordinarily practical and often highly valued. If your software aids in streamlining a complex process, a checklist for that process, or a template they can utilise, can serve as an excellent nurturing piece. It addresses a small, tangible problem and subtly conveys your expertise.

Email mini-courses or drip campaigns: this involves sending a series of short, educational emails over several days or weeks, each building on the previous one, centred on a specific topic pertinent to your ICP's challenges. It's an excellent way to deliver value in digestible portions.

Short explainer videos: you don't need a professional film crew. A clear, concise video (even a simple screen recording with good audio) explaining a complex concept, demonstrating how a specific feature of your early product addresses a particular pain point, or sharing a quick insight from the founder can be very effective. Keep them short and focused.

Credibility-building content is also crucial when you're a new, relatively unknown entity. This type of content helps prospects trust that you know what you're doing and that your solution has merit.

Case studies: even if you only have a few early users or beta testers, try to document their stories (with their permission, of course). Focus on the challenges they faced, the approach you took (even if the solution was still evolving) and any initial positive outcomes they experienced. A simple, honest narrative can be very compelling.

Testimonials: a short, genuine quote from a happy early user can be incredibly powerful. You can sprinkle these into your emails, on your website or your social media. Video testimonials, even brief and unpolished ones, can be even more impactful.

Founder Q&A sessions (live or recorded): hosting a brief webinar or recording a video where you, as the founder, address common questions or concerns related to your industry or solution can build transparency and trust. It demonstrates that you're accessible and knowledgeable.

As leads progress further down the funnel and nearer to a decision, more product-focused content can be introduced, always framed in the context of addressing their specific problems.

Targeted feature highlights: rather than a generic product tour, develop short pieces of content (an email, a one-page PDF, a brief video) that demonstrate how one specific feature of your product directly addresses a pain point known to affect that lead segment.

Comparison sheets (used ethically): if prospects are evaluating your solution against others (or considering the 'do nothing' status quo), a simple sheet that fairly outlines your unique advantages and differentiators, tailored to their needs, can be beneficial. Emphasise how your approach is distinct and superior for them. Always bear in mind, just like an advertisement, your content must be legal, decent, honest and truthful.

Webinar recordings (if applicable): if you've hosted an educational webinar that subtly showcases your product, providing the recording to nurtured leads can be an excellent way for them to learn more at their own pace.

Create Once, Repurpose Often

Now, how do you actually create this content when you're already stretched thin? The lean startup mentality applies here as well. It's about being smart and resourceful.

One of the most powerful techniques is repurposing. Don't think of each piece of content as a one-off effort. A single in-depth blog post can be broken down into several key takeaways for social media updates, become the script for a short video, be expanded into a chapter of a downloadable guide or provide the core ideas for an email nurturing sequence. Always be thinking, 'How can I use this idea or this piece of research in multiple ways?'

Curation with commentary is another time-saver. You don't always have to create everything from scratch. Sharing a highly relevant article or report from a reputable third-party source, along with your own insightful commentary explaining why it matters to your audience or how it relates to the problems you solve, can provide significant value. This positions you as a helpful filter and a thoughtful leader in your space.

Remember, as the founder, you are the primary subject matter expert. Your unique insights, passion for the problems you solve and authentic voice are powerful content assets. Don't feel the need to sound like a corporate marketing department. Often, a direct, honest and slightly informal tone can be more engaging and build more trust than overly polished prose. Share your journey, learnings and vision.

Keep your content simple and relentlessly clear. Your audience is busy. They want actionable advice and easily digestible information. Avoid unnecessary jargon and overly academic language. Get to the point and make it obvious how your content can help them.

There are numerous free or low-cost tools available to assist you with basic content creation. Canva is excellent for designing simple graphics, social media visuals or formatting PDFs. Your smartphone can capture surprisingly good video and there are various free or affordable mobile video-editing apps available.

For email marketing, services such as Mailchimp, Sendinblue or Moosend offer free tiers that are perfectly sufficient for getting started with nurturing sequences.

Educate, Don't Pitch

Once you've created (or curated) your valuable content, you must present it to your leads. Sending random pieces of content sporadically is unlikely to be effective. You require a distribution strategy, primarily focused on nurturing those who have already expressed some interest.

Email marketing sequences serve as the backbone of B2B lead nurturing. This involves establishing a series of automated (or semi-automated) emails that are sent to a lead over a period following a particular action (e.g. downloading a resource, signing up for your newsletter or simply becoming a 'warm lead' in your system).

Segmentation is key: Not all your leads share the same interests or are at the same stage. If possible, segment your leads based on their initial interest, industry, the problem they are trying to solve or how they entered your pipeline. This will allow you to tailor your email nurturing sequences with content that is most relevant to each segment. Bombarding leads with irrelevant content is a surefire way to ensure your emails are deleted before they are ever opened. Invest time in segmenting your leads; it will pay off in the end.

Personalisation matters: go beyond merely using their [First Name]. If your CRM or spreadsheet captures it, reference their company, industry, a challenge they mentioned in a previous conversation or the specific piece of content they initially engaged with. This demonstrates that you are paying attention.

Each email should provide value: avoid sending 'checking in' emails.

Each message in your sequence ought to offer a new piece of helpful content, a valuable insight or an invitation to another useful resource.

Have a clear Call to Action (CTA): what do you want them to do after reading your email? It might be reading a blog post, downloading a guide, watching a short video or, as they warm up, scheduling a brief call. Ensure the CTA is obvious and easy to follow.

While email is central, leverage your social media platforms (primarily LinkedIn) for nurturing as well. Share your more in-depth nurturing content (such as blog posts or guides) with your network. If you notice a prospect asking a question or discussing a challenge in a LinkedIn group or on their feed that your content addresses, you can thoughtfully share a link to your resource in a comment or a direct message. 'Hi [Name], I saw you were asking about X. I recently wrote a short piece on that which might offer some helpful perspectives: [link]. Hope it's useful!'

Your website or blog should serve as a central hub for your nurturing content. Make it easy for those leads exploring your site to find your articles, guides and other resources. This reinforces your expertise and provides a valuable library they can access on their own terms.

Don't forget the power of directly sharing specific content in your sales follow-ups. If, during a discovery call, a prospect mentions a particular challenge or asks a specific question and you have a blog post or guide that addresses it directly, sending that to them afterwards is a highly relevant and valuable nurturing touch. 'Following up on our conversation earlier, you mentioned you were struggling with Y. Here's an article I wrote that offers a few strategies for tackling just that: [link].'

Lead nurturing isn't just about pushing content at people; it's also about fostering engagement around that content. When you share something on LinkedIn or your blog and someone comments or asks a question, respond! Engage in the discussion. This turns passive content consumption into an active dialogue, further building the relationship and your credibility.

Personalised check-ins that aren't solely focused on pushing content can also be part of your nurturing strategy. A brief, sincere email enquiring how they're getting on with a particular challenge they mentioned or sharing a quick, relevant observation without a hard sell, can keep you top of mind in a positive way.

Measuring the success of your early nurturing efforts may feel less tangible than tracking direct sales, but it's still crucial to know what's working.

For email nurturing, monitor basic metrics like open rates and click-through rates. Are people opening your emails? Are they clicking on the links to your content? This provides you with insights into how engaging your subject lines and email copy are. Track content downloads or views. Are individuals accessing the guides, checklists or articles you're sharing? Pay attention to qualitative feedback. Are leads mentioning your content in their conversations with you? 'Thanks for sending that article on X, it was really helpful.' Are they asking more informed questions as a result of the information you've provided? These are strong indicators that your nurturing is effective.

Ultimately, the most important metric is how many nurtured leads progress to the next stage in your sales process. How many request a demo, agree to a more in-depth consultation or start asking buying questions after being in your nurturing flow?

Don't expect every lead to engage with every piece of content. The goal is to provide a steady stream of value so that when they are ready to take the next step, your startup is the one they think of first because you've been consistently helpful and have built trust. This brings us to a critical question: when is a nurtured lead ready for a more direct sales conversation? How do you know when to shift from providing educational content to actively trying to schedule a demo or close a deal? Look for buying signals. These can be explicit (e.g. they reply to a nurturing email asking for pricing or a demo) or implicit (e.g. your website analytics show they've repeatedly visited your pricing page, they've downloaded a 'bottom-of-the-funnel' piece of content like a detailed product comparison or they start asking very specific questions about how your solution would work (for their exact scenario).

Some businesses use lead scoring systems to track these signals automatically but as a founder, you can do this more intuitively or with a very simple points system in your spreadsheet. For example, downloading a guide might be 5 points, visiting the pricing page 10 points, requesting a demo 50 points. When a lead reaches a certain threshold, it signals they're 'sales-qualified' and ready for a more direct sales approach.

Content marketing for lead nurturing is an investment of your time and intellect, but it's one that pays significant dividends for a B2B startup. It allows you to stay engaged with leads who aren't ready to buy today, build your reputation as a trusted expert and ensure that when the time is right, you're the one they turn to. It's the patient, value-driven approach that builds sustainable pipelines and loyal early customers. It is one of the major ways that your prospects will see you as a 'knowledge leader' and this is where you want to be.

KEY TAKEAWAYS

- Content builds long-term trust and positions you as a credible problem-solver.

- Use content to stay top of mind during longer sales cycles.

- Focus on what your customer needs to learn, not what you want to say.

FOUNDER'S FIELDWORK

Define Three Key Content Themes: choose three subjects your ideal customer cares about, or problems they need to solve (e.g. compliance, automation, team productivity).

Write One Educational Post: create a LinkedIn post or blog that solves a common customer problem or misconception.

Create a Content Calendar: plan out one piece of content per week for the next month (topics, format and distribution channel).

Build a 'Low-Effort' Content Stack: repurpose one blog into a LinkedIn post, email and short checklist.

Email Nurture Starter: draft a three-email sequence for leads who aren't ready yet – focus on insight, not urgency.

Tag and Track Engagement: note which leads interact with your content – these are warm contacts worth re-engaging.

Chapter seventeen

COLD OUTREACH: MAKING IT WORK FOR YOU

'The cold call is not dead. It just needs to be smarter.' – Trish Bertuzzi

Personalised, Precise and Polite

All right, let's discuss a sales activity that often receives a bad reputation, sometimes deservedly so: cold outreach. The very phrase might evoke images of relentless spammers, generic email blasts or awkward, unsolicited phone calls. For many entrepreneurs, especially those who take pride in building something valuable and authentic, the notion of reaching out to someone who doesn't know you from Adam can feel uncomfortable, intrusive, or even a tad desperate. But here's the unvarnished truth: when you're a startup founder striving to get your B2B venture off the ground, cold outreach, when approached thoughtfully and strategically, isn't merely an option; it's frequently a vital necessity. This chapter aims to strip away the sleaze and show you how to make cold outreach work for you, leveraging your unique position as a founder to create genuine connections and open doors that might otherwise remain firmly shut.

Consider it this way. You've built something you believe in and you know it can solve a real problem for a specific type of business, but those businesses aren't yet aware of your existence. How will they find out? While inbound strategies like content marketing (which we've discussed for lead nurturing) are fantastic for the long game, they require time to yield results. In the crucial early days, you often can't afford to simply wait for the phone to ring or for leads to appear magically in your inbox. Cold outreach is your proactive way of saying, 'Hello, I exist and I might have something that can genuinely help you.' It's about initiating valuable conversations, not merely pushing your product.

The key distinction between the cold outreach we're championing here and the type that gives the practice a bad name is straightforward: value and relevance. It's not about broadcasting your message far and wide in the hopes that a tiny percentage sticks. It's about precise targeting, deep personalisation and providing a genuine reason for your prospect to pay attention. As a founder, you're uniquely positioned to do this. You're not a detached salesperson operating from a script; you're the architect of the solution, motivated by a deep understanding of the problem. Your authenticity and passion, when channelled effectively, can enable your cold outreach to stand out.

Before you even consider sending your first cold email or making your initial tentative call, certain foundational elements must be firmly in place. Attempting cold outreach without these is akin to setting sail without a map or compass – you'll drift aimlessly and likely end up frustrated.

Firstly, absolute clarity on your Ideal Customer Profile (ICP), as meticulously detailed in Chapter Five, is non-negotiable. Who precisely are you trying to reach? What are their specific job titles, industries, company sizes and, most importantly, their acute pain points that your solution addresses? If you can't answer this with precision, your outreach will be fundamentally unfocused.

Secondly, your Unique Value Proposition (UVP), crafted in Chapter Three and woven into a narrative in Chapter Four, must be razor-sharp. Why should this specific ICP care about what you have to offer, especially when they have never heard of you? Your UVP forms the core of your outreach message.

Thirdly, you need at least a basic professional online presence. This typically means a well-optimised LinkedIn profile (as discussed in Chapter Fifteen on Social Selling) where prospects can verify that you are a genuine, credible individual. A simple, professional-looking website or landing page for your startup, even if it is just one page, also provides legitimacy and is essential.

Finally, you need a system, however rudimentary, for tracking your outreach efforts. This could be a simple spreadsheet or a free CRM tier, as mentioned in Chapter Thirteen on Lead Generation. You must keep track of who you have contacted, when, with what message, and any responses. Without this, chaos will swiftly ensue.

With these prerequisites in place, let us consider the channels. For a lean startup founder, the primary weapon in the cold outreach arsenal is typically email. It is asynchronous, allowing prospects to respond at their convenience. It can be personalised effectively and permits you to convey a significant amount of information concisely. LinkedIn serves as an excellent complementary channel, not just for initial research or connection requests but also for direct messaging (InMail if you have it, or messages to 2nd/3rd-degree connections who are 'open profile' or in shared groups).

The cold call poses a tougher proposition in the modern B2B landscape, often with lower success rates and requiring specific skills and resilience. While we shall touch on it, for most founders beginning their journey, a well-crafted email or LinkedIn message sequence is likely to be a more efficient use of your limited time.

Openers That Open Doors

Let us delve deeply into crafting cold emails that people genuinely open, read and consider responding to. This is an art form that balances brevity, value and personalisation.

The subject line represents your first and, arguably, biggest hurdle. It acts as the gatekeeper to your entire message. Your prospect's inbox is a battlefield of competing priorities. Your subject line must be compelling enough to earn a click, but not so misleading or clickbaity that it immediately erodes trust. Keep it succinct (many email clients truncate lengthy subjects, especially on mobile). Personalisation can be effective here – mentioning their company name, a mutual connection or a highly relevant pain point. While curiosity can be beneficial, clarity is often more important. Avoid spammy words, excessive capitalisation, or strings of exclamation marks. Think: 'Quick question about [Their Company]'s approach to [Relevant Pain Point]' or 'Idea for improving [Specific Metric] at [Their Company]'.

Once they've opened your email, the opening line is critical. It must immediately reinforce that this isn't a generic blast. This is where your research pays off. Reference something specific you learned about them or their company: 'I was impressed by your recent article on X,' or 'Saw that [Their Company] recently achieved Y – congratulations!' or 'John Doe suggested I reach out...' This demonstrates that you've invested time and aren't just another random sender.

Next, you need to very succinctly bridge to your ultra-concise value proposition. You don't have room for your full narrative here. You need to quickly connect the dots between a likely problem they have (based on your ICP research) and the core benefit your solution offers. For example: 'Many [Their Job Title] in the [Their Industry] sector tell us they struggle with [Specific Problem]. We help them achieve [Specific Benefit/Outcome] by [Briefly, How You Do It].' Focus entirely on their world and their potential gain.

Your Call to Action (CTA) must be crystal clear and, importantly, low-friction. You're not asking for marriage on the first date. You're not trying to close the sale in the first email. Your primary goal for initial cold outreach is usually to simply start a conversation or secure a brief exploratory call. Make your request easy to say 'yes' to. Instead of 'Can I schedule a one-hour demo?' try 'Would you be open to a brief fifteen-minute call next week to explore if this might be relevant for your team?' or 'Is this a challenge you're currently prioritising? If so, I have a couple of initial thoughts I'd be happy to share.' Offering specific, limited time slots can also reduce back-and-forth: 'Would Tuesday at 2 pm or Wednesday at 10 am work for a quick chat?'

Your email signature should be professional and reinforce your credibility. Include your full name, title (Founder at [Your Startup]), company name, a link to your simple website or landing page and a link to your LinkedIn profile. This enables them to easily check you out if they are intrigued.

Now, let's discuss personalisation at scale – the lean startup edition. You cannot possibly write every single cold email from scratch if you are attempting to reach a reasonable number of prospects. This is where templates can be useful, but only as a starting framework. The key is to identify specific sections of your template that must be deeply personalised for each prospect. Consider the 80/20 rule: perhaps 80% of the email comprises a well-crafted core message about the problem/solution, while 20% (the opening line, the specific reference to their company, perhaps a slight tweak to the value proposition) is unique to them. This targeted personalisation makes all the difference. Avoid merge fields that scream 'This is a mass email!' if they are not perfectly implemented. For example, we have all seen and received numerous cold outreach emails that do not even get our names right and they are precisely what the delete key was made for.

The tone of your cold outreach should be professional yet approachable, respectful and empathetic to the fact that you are interrupting their day. Convey confidence in what you offer, but avoid arrogance or pushiness. As the founder, your genuine passion can come through but temper it with a clear focus on their needs.

LinkedIn provides another avenue for direct cold outreach, particularly through InMail (if you have a Premium or Sales Navigator account) or by messaging connections. The principles are quite similar to cold email: keep it personalised, value-driven and concise. Referring to shared connections, common groups or their recent LinkedIn activity ('I saw you commented on X post and it resonated because...') can be effective icebreakers. Given the nature of LinkedIn messaging, brevity is even more important here. Get to the point quickly but politely. Your CTA might be to connect for a brief virtual coffee or to direct them to a valuable resource you have shared.

What about the dreaded cold call? For many founders, especially those without prior sales experience, this is the most intimidating form of outreach. It has a high rejection rate and requires significant resilience. However, for certain industries or very high-value, meticulously researched prospects, a well-executed cold call might still have a place, although it is generally a lower-leverage activity for a lean startup compared to targeted email or LinkedIn outreach.

If you do decide to try cold calling, preparation is everything. Don't just dial and hope. Have a clear objective for the call; usually, it's not to sell, but to introduce yourself, briefly state your value proposition and ask for a few minutes of their time for a proper follow-up meeting. Develop a 'mini-script' or a set of talking points, not to read verbatim, but to keep you focused. Your opening needs to be incredibly concise and grab attention positively within seconds: 'Hi [Prospect Name], this is [Your Name], founder of [Your Startup]. The reason for my call is that we help companies like yours in the [Their Industry] sector to solve [Specific Problem]. Would you have a brief moment to see if exploring this further might make sense?'

Be prepared for gatekeepers (receptionists, assistants). Treat them with the utmost respect; they can be powerful allies or insurmountable barriers. Clearly state your name, company and whom you're trying to reach and politely ask for their help.

If you manage to connect with the prospect, anticipate immediate objections ('I'm busy', 'Not interested', 'We already have a solution). Have brief, respectful responses ready but avoid arguing. Often, your goal is simply to secure a commitment for a scheduled follow-up call during which they've set aside time to listen. If you receive a firm 'no', thank them for their time and move on gracefully.

Follow-Up without the Fatigue
Regardless of the channel you use, follow-up is often where the magic occurs. Very few positive responses stem from the very first touchpoint. People are busy; your message might be missed or the timing may not be suitable. A systematic, polite follow-up cadence is

essential. We discussed prospecting cadences in Chapter Fourteen; for cold outreach, this entails a series of 3–5 touchpoints over a few weeks. Each follow-up should ideally provide a new piece of value or a slightly different angle. Don't simply bump your original email with 'Just checking in'. Instead, consider: 'Following up on my previous email, I thought this short article on [Relevant Topic] might be interesting to you' or 'Since I last reached out, we helped a company in a similar space achieve [Brief, Compelling Result]. Might be worth a quick chat if that's a priority for you too.'

Vary your follow-up channels if appropriate. If your first touch was via email, perhaps a gentle LinkedIn message or connection request could serve as a follow-up. The key is persistence without becoming a nuisance. If you've made several polite, value-added attempts and received no response, it's generally time to respectfully pause outreach to that individual and focus your energy elsewhere.

To do all this effectively, especially as a solo founder, you'll want a few simple, affordable tools of the trade.

Your standard email client (Gmail, Outlook) serves as your primary sending tool.

For finding email addresses, services like Hunter.io, Skrapp.io, or Apollo.io often offer free tiers for a limited number of lookups per month. Always use these ethically and responsibly, focusing on publicly listed business contact information and complying with the laws of the country where the prospect resides. LinkedIn, as mentioned, is your main research and connection platform; Sales Navigator is a substantial upgrade if your budget eventually allows but the free version is more than adequate for starting out.

For tracking your outreach, a simple spreadsheet or a free CRM (like HubSpot CRM's free tier or Zoho CRM's free tier) is indispensable. Make a note of who you contacted, when, the message sent, any response received and your next follow-up date.

Optional, but sometimes helpful, are email tracking tools (like HubSpot Sales Hub free tools or Mailtrack for Gmail) that can show you if your emails have been opened or links clicked. This can provide some insight into engagement but use this information ethically – don't call someone the moment you see they opened your email, as that can feel intrusive.

When you do receive responses (or non-responses), how should you react? If you get a positive response agreeing to a call, fantastic! Reply promptly to confirm the time, send a calendar invite and do a little extra preparation for that specific conversation.

If you receive a neutral response ('Not interested right now', 'Bad timing', 'Send me more info') or an objection, this is where your objection handling skills (Chapter Eleven) come into play. Acknowledge their point, perhaps ask a gentle clarifying question and see if there's an opening. Sometimes 'Send me more info' is a polite brush-off but it can also be a genuine request. If so, send a concise, highly relevant piece of information, not your entire product brochure.

If you receive no response at all after your follow-up cadence, don't despair and don't take it personally. There are myriad reasons why someone might not reply. Move on. You can always revisit that prospect much later (months down the line) with a significantly different value proposition or a major company update.

If you receive an unsubscribe request or a genuinely negative reply, handle it with complete professionalism. Remove them from your outreach list immediately and, if appropriate, offer a brief, polite apology for any unwelcome intrusion. Your reputation is important.

It's also vital to be conscious of the legal and ethical considerations of cold outreach. Regulations such as GDPR (in Europe) and CAN-SPAM (in the US) outline rules regarding unsolicited commercial electronic messages. While the specifics can be complex, the core principle generally revolves around transparency, honouring opt-outs and avoiding deception. Always clearly identify yourself and your company. Provide an easy way for individuals to opt-out of future communications. Crucially, direct your outreach towards individuals and businesses where you have a genuine, well-researched belief that your offering could truly be valuable to them. This isn't solely about compliance; it's about sound business practice. Your aim is to be a welcome problem-solver, not an unwelcome pest.

Finally, treat your cold outreach efforts as an ongoing experiment. Iterate and improve. You're a lean startup and this approach applies to your sales tactics as well. Track some basic metrics: what percentage of your emails are opened? What percentage receive a reply? Of those replies, how many are positive or lead to a conversation? You don't need complex analytics. Even a simple tally can provide significant insights.

Experiment with A/B testing various subject lines using small batches of emails. Assess which one achieves a better open rate. Try different CTAs. Does requesting a ten-minute call perform better than a twenty-minute request? Does providing a specific piece of content as a next step yield greater engagement? The feedback you receive, even in the form of rejections or silence, counts as data. Perhaps your targeting is slightly misaligned. Maybe your value proposition isn't resonating as clearly as you believed. Or perhaps the pain point you assume your ICP has isn't actually their most pressing concern. As the founder, you are in a unique position to leverage this direct market feedback and swiftly iterate on your messaging, targeting and even your product priorities.

Cold outreach, when approached with intelligence, empathy and persistence, can be an exceptionally powerful tool for a startup founder. It enables you to take charge of your lead generation, engage directly with your target market and begin building the relationships that will drive your company's growth, one carefully crafted message at a time.

KEY TAKEAWAYS

- Cold outreach still works – if it's relevant, respectful and sharp.

- Lead with insight or a question that proves you've done your research.

- Follow-up is where most results happen – don't stop after one try.

FOUNDER'S FIELDWORK

Build Your First Cold Email Template: include a personalised hook, pain point, short pitch and clear CTA (call to action).

Email Clarity Test: send a cold email to a peer and ask them: what's the problem I solve? Would you reply?

Send Ten Emails with Variations: A/B test different subject lines and opening lines. Track open and reply rates.

Record a Sixty-Second Cold Pitch Video: try sending this to leads instead of an email, track engagement.

Timebox Outreach: block two thirty-minute sessions per week dedicated solely to cold prospecting, no multitasking.

Create a 'Follow-Up Ladder': draught a three to five message sequence you can use to stay in touch with cold leads over time.

Chapter eighteen

NETWORKING AND BUILDING STRATEGIC PARTNERSHIPS

'Your network is your net worth.' – Porter Gale

Intentional Networking for Impact

Thus far, we've discussed extensively about directly finding and engaging potential customers. That's the bread and butter of early sales. But what if you could amplify your reach, gain credibility by association and even create new avenues to market without necessarily doing all the heavy lifting yourself?

This is where the often misunderstood, yet incredibly potent, duo of networking and strategic partnerships comes into play. For you, the founder navigating the choppy waters of a startup, these aren't merely buzzwords; they are force multipliers. This chapter aims to demystify these concepts and show you how to weave them into your lean sales strategy to open doors you might not even know exist.

Many entrepreneurs hear 'networking' and picture stuffy rooms filled with people awkwardly exchanging business cards and delivering forced elevator pitches. If that's your image, let's repaint it. Effective networking, particularly for a startup founder, isn't about collecting the most contacts; it's about making genuine connections. It's about building a web of relationships with individuals who might not be your direct customers today but who could become advocates, offer invaluable advice, provide referrals or even transform into those crucial early strategic partners. Think of it as building your business's social capital.

Why is this so vital when you're lean and mean? Because a strong network can provide shortcuts and credibility that are hard to buy. A warm introduction from a trusted contact is infinitely more powerful than a cold email. A recommendation from an industry peer can lend your fledgling startup instant legitimacy. And a well-chosen strategic partner can give you access to a whole new pool of potential customers. Your mindset going into this should always be one of mutual benefit and a long-term view. It's less about 'What can you do for me?' and more about 'How can we help each other?' and 'What interesting things can we learn together?' Before you dive in, it's crucial to be selective about where you invest your precious networking time. You cannot be everywhere and not all ponds are stocked with the fish you're looking for. Your Ideal Customer Profile (ICP) and your understanding of your industry should guide your choices.

Online networking offers a wealth of low-cost opportunities. We've touched on LinkedIn for social selling but for deeper networking LinkedIn Groups that are highly relevant to your ICP's industry or specific challenges can be goldmines. Don't just join; participate thoughtfully. Ask insightful questions, offer helpful answers (without overtly selling) and engage in genuine discussions. This is where you can move beyond just a connection to being seen as a knowledgeable and helpful peer.

Beyond LinkedIn, look for niche industry forums or online communities. These are often places where professionals gather to discuss specific problems and solutions in more detail. Your authentic participation here can quickly establish your expertise.

Virtual events, webinars and online conferences have surged in popularity, with many offering free or very affordable access. Seek out events that your target audience or potential partners are likely to attend. Many platforms now feature virtual networking lounges, Q&A sessions with speakers and attendee lists that you can (ethically and respectfully) utilise for targeted follow-ups.

Remember to leverage your alumni networks. Whether from university or previous workplaces, these connections often share a pre-existing common ground, making outreach warmer and more receptive.

When circumstances allow and it is appropriate for your industry, offline networking still retains value, though you must be even more selective due to time and cost constraints. Local business meetups can be beneficial for building community and locating local service providers or even early clients if your ICP is geographically focused. Niche industry conferences require a greater commitment but if you choose wisely (perhaps opting for smaller, more focused events where you can engage in more meaningful conversations) they can be incredibly valuable for deep immersion and connecting with key players. Chambers of Commerce could be relevant if your business targets a broad spectrum of local enterprises. Additionally, workshops and seminars in your field or related areas can also serve as networking opportunities.

The key is to ask, 'Where do the people I want to connect with (potential clients, referrers, partners, mentors) genuinely spend their time and seek information?' Focus your energy there. It's better to be an active, recognised participant in one or two relevant communities than a silent ghost in twenty.

Once you're in the right place, whether online or offline, how do you forge meaningful connections? Preparation is your ally. If it's an event, review the attendee list or speaker lineup beforehand. You will usually find this in a media pack provided by the event organisers. Request this and ensure you receive it, as it will help you determine if the event is likely to be of value. Identify a few key individuals you'd like to connect with. If it's an online forum, take some time to observe and understand the community's tone and common topics before you engage. Have a clear, concise way to explain who you are and what your startup does (your elevator pitch, adapted for a conversational setting – Chapter Four).

The golden rule of networking interactions is to listen more than you talk. Be genuinely curious about the other person. Ask open-ended questions about their work, their challenges, their interests. People generally enjoy talking about themselves and their passions. When they feel heard and understood, rapport builds naturally. Your aim in an initial networking conversation is not to sell but to explore if there's a basis for a mutually beneficial connection. Look for common ground, shared interests or areas where you might be able to offer them some small piece of help or insight, even if it's just connecting them with someone else in your network.

When it's your turn to speak, be concise and concentrate on the problem you solve and the people you assist. If they show interest, fantastic. If not, then don't press it. The 'How can I help you?' mentality is incredibly powerful. Even if they aren't a direct prospect or partner, they may know someone who is. If you focus on being a valuable connector for others, that goodwill often returns to you.

Gracefully entering and exiting conversations is a practical skill. In a group, listen first, then find a natural moment to contribute. If approaching someone directly (e.g. at an event), a simple 'Hi, I'm [Your Name] from [YourStartup]. I was intrigued by your comment about X...' can work. When it's time to move on, a polite 'It was great chatting with you, [Their Name]. I'd love to connect on LinkedIn to stay in touch,' ensures a smooth exit. Exchanging contact information should be straightforward. Having your LinkedIn QR code handy on your phone is often quicker than fumbling for cards.

From Contacts to Collaborators
The most critical aspect of networking – and the one most frequently overlooked – is the follow-up. A brief meeting or a new LinkedIn connection is just the starting point. To transform that interaction into a genuine relationship, you need to follow up within a day or two. Send a personalised email or LinkedIn message. Refer to something specific from your conversation to demonstrate you were listening. For example: 'Hi [Name], great to connect with you at the [Event/Online Group] yesterday. I particularly enjoyed our chat about [Specific Topic]. Here's that article I mentioned on [Relevant Subject] that I thought you might find interesting. Hope to stay in touch.' Your

follow-up shouldn't be a sales pitch. It should focus on reinforcing the connection and providing further value.

Building and nurturing your network is an ongoing effort; it's not something you undertake for a week and then forget. Consider how you can remain top-of-mind authentically. This might involve regularly sharing valuable content on LinkedIn (as discussed in Chapter Fifteen), sending a brief note to congratulate a contact on a new role or achievement, making a helpful introduction between two individuals in your network who could benefit from knowing each other or occasionally sharing an article or resource you believe a specific contact would find particularly useful, accompanied by a personal note. Your simple CRM or even a dedicated section in your spreadsheet can be invaluable for keeping track of key contacts, what you discussed and when you last interacted. Remember, the aim is to consistently provide value, not just to reach out when you require something.

As your network expands and your understanding of the market deepens, you will begin to identify individuals or companies that could transcend casual contacts. These are your potential strategic partners. For a startup, a strategic partnership is a formal or informal collaboration with another business, where you work together for mutual benefit, often to reach a wider audience, offer a more complete solution or gain credibility. It's about identifying complementary strengths.

What does a strategic partnership look like for a lean entrepreneur? It can take many forms:

Referral Partnerships: you agree to refer clients to one another. This is most effective when your services are complementary and target a similar ICP, yet are non-competing. For instance, if you provide specialised software for marketing agencies, you might partner with a consultant who offers strategic marketing advice to those same agencies.

Complementary Service Providers: you bundle your offering with that of another business to provide a more comprehensive solution.

Perhaps your software manages one part of a workflow, while another company's software oversees a different part. Integrating or co-marketing these can be a powerful strategy.

Co-Marketing Initiatives: you collaborate on a piece of content (such as a webinar, a joint research report or a co-authored guide), a joint event or a shared social media campaign to engage each other's audiences. This can be a highly cost-effective approach to expanding your reach.

Technology Integrations: if your product is software, integrating with other popular tools that your ICP already uses can make your solution significantly more attractive and engaging. These often begin as informal collaborations and can evolve into more formal partnerships.

Affiliate Partnerships: you pay a commission to partners who successfully refer paying customers to you. This is more common once you have established a proven sales process and clear metrics.

Identifying potential partners often occurs organically through your networking activities. Someone with whom you've built a rapport might have a business that perfectly complements yours. You may also proactively research companies that serve your ICP with non-competing solutions. Look for businesses whose values align with yours, that have a solid reputation and that demonstrate a similar commitment to customer success.

When you think you've found a potential partner, how do you approach them? This isn't a cold sales pitch; it's an invitation to explore a mutually beneficial collaboration. Do your homework: understand their business, their offerings and their audience as thoroughly as you can. Then, reach out with a clear, concise proposal. Explain who you are, what you do and why you believe a partnership could specifically benefit them. 'Hi [Potential Partner Name], I've been following [Their Company] for a while and am very impressed with your work in [Their Area]. We at [Your Startup] provide [Your Solution] to a similar audience and I see a strong potential for us to help each other by [Specific Partnership Idea – e.g. referring clients, co-hosting a webinar on X topic]. Would you be open to a brief chat to explore this?'

The initial conversation should focus on exploring possibilities and gauging interest. What are their strategic goals? Where do they see potential synergies? What are their concerns? Concentrate on building a clear picture of the mutual benefit. If they can't see a distinct advantage for themselves, the partnership is unlikely to take off or be sustainable.

For early-stage startups, it's often prudent to start small with any partnership. Instead of attempting to negotiate a complex, multi-faceted agreement from day one, suggest a pilot programme or a single, well-defined collaborative project. This allows you both to test the waters, see how well you work together and demonstrate value before committing substantial resources. For example, you might co-host one webinar first or establish a simple reciprocal referral process for a trial period.

Even if the partnership is initially informal, it's important to clarify expectations, roles and responsibilities. A simple email summary of your agreements can help prevent misunderstandings. If the partnership involves revenue sharing or more significant commitments, a basic written agreement is advisable, even if it's just a short, plain-language document. (We'll cover more formal contract management in Chapter Twenty). Once a partnership is established, it requires nurturing, just like any other relationship. Regular communication is key. Keep your partners updated on what's happening with your business (especially if it's relevant to them). Check in to see how things are going on their end. Look for ways to support them, even beyond the strict terms of the partnership. Are they launching a new product? Offer to share it with your network. Are they looking for a speaker for an event? Perhaps you or someone you know could fit the bill.

Trust, Generosity and Long-Term Thinking

As the founder, you are often the primary champion of these early partnerships. Your personal involvement and commitment can significantly impact their success. Track the results of your collaborations. How many referrals did you exchange? How many leads did that joint webinar generate? This data helps you understand what's working and where to focus your efforts.

Naturally, there are pitfalls to avoid in both networking and partnerships. A common networking mistake is being purely transactional – only reaching out when you want something or collecting contacts like trophies without building genuine connections. Another is spreading yourself too thin, trying to be involved in too many areas and, consequently, failing to make a meaningful impact in any. Failing to follow up is perhaps the biggest networking sin; a connection made but not nurtured is a wasted opportunity. Many also become discouraged by expecting immediate results. Genuine relationships and fruitful partnerships take time to build.

When it comes to strategic partnerships, a key pitfall is entering them without clear goals or proper due diligence. Just because a company looks good on paper doesn't mean they'll be a good partner in practice. Lack of alignment on values, target audience or levels of commitment can doom a partnership. Another mistake is underestimating the time needed to manage and nurture a partnership effectively; it's not a 'set it and forget it' activity.

Networking and building strategic partnerships fundamentally involve creating a supportive ecosystem around your startup. It's about recognising that you don't have to go it alone. By investing time in cultivating genuine relationships and seeking collaborations where everyone benefits, you, the entrepreneurial salesperson, can significantly expand your reach, enhance your credibility and create new pathways to growth, while learning from and contributing to the broader business community.

KEY TAKEAWAYS

- Strategic networking opens doors to warm leads, partnerships and referrals.

- Quality trumps quantity – focus on depth, not breadth.

- Give value first to build credibility and trust.

FOUNDER'S FIELDWORK

Map Your Ecosystem: list five adjacent services or platforms that target the same audience as you but aren't direct competitors.

Reach Out to One Potential Partner: propose a simple value exchange: shared content, co-promotion or warm intros.

Attend One Networking Event: online or offline; commit to asking three meaningful questions per person you meet.

Create a Personal Connection Bank: keep notes on key contacts: how you met, their business and something personal; a spreadsheet is all you need at this stage.

Offer Three Intros before Asking for One: build goodwill and social capital by proactively helping others in your network.

PART 4

CLOSING AND GROWING

This is where deals are won or lost. Learn how to close with confidence, negotiate effectively and build long-term client relationships that sustain the revenue flow. It's not about tricks – it's about trust, timing and value. You'll move from 'maybe' to 'signed' without feeling pushy or salesy.

Chapter nineteen

THE ART OF THE CLOSE – PROVEN CLOSING TECHNIQUES

'"Always be closing" is outdated – today it's "always be helping".' – Daniel H. Pink (paraphrased)

Creating Conditions to Close Naturally

You've done the hard yards. You've built something you believe in, identified who it's for, listened intently to their needs and articulated your value proposition with passion and clarity. The prospect seems interested; they're nodding along and the objections, if any, have been addressed. Now what?

This is the moment when many entrepreneurs, especially those new to sales, can feel a knot in their stomach. It's the close – that point where you transition from discussing possibilities to asking for a commitment. For some, 'closing' conjures images of aggressive tactics and high-pressure manoeuvres. But for you, the founder selling your own B2B offering, it's nothing of the sort. It's simply the natural, logical culmination of a value-driven conversation, a moment where you help a genuinely interested prospect make a good decision for their business.

This chapter is about demystifying the art of the close. We're not going to arm you with manipulative tricks or phrases designed to corner someone. Instead, we'll explore proven, ethical closing techniques that align with the lean, founder-led sales approach.

These methods aim to make it easy for the right prospects to say 'yes', feeling confident and positive about their decision to partner with your startup. It's about guiding, not goading.

Your mindset as you approach the close is absolutely critical. If you feel apologetic or hesitant about asking for the sale, your prospect will sense it. Your confidence shouldn't stem from arrogance but from a deep-seated belief in the value your product or service delivers. You've done your homework; you understand their problem and you genuinely believe you can help them. Asking for their business is simply the next logical step in that helping process. Think of it as opening a door for them, not pushing them through it. Persistence, rooted in this belief, is also key – not the annoying, badgering kind, but the professional resolve to see the conversation through to a clear outcome.

Before you can even consider deploying a closing technique, you need to be attuned to the signals that your prospect is warming up and nearing a decision. These buying signals, both verbal and non-verbal, are your cues that the timing might be right to guide the conversation towards a commitment. Paying attention to these is crucial because attempting to close too early can feel abrupt, while waiting too long might cause the prospect's interest to cool or allow doubts to creep in.

Verbal buying signals are often quite direct. Prospects might start asking detailed questions about the practicalities of moving forward. Watch for phrases like, 'So, what are the next steps if we want to proceed?' or 'How long would it take to get this implemented?' Questions about specific pricing tiers, payment terms, contract lengths or customisation options also indicate they're seriously considering what you're offering. They might start using 'we' or 'us' when talking about using your product or service, such as, 'How would we integrate this with our existing system?' or 'This would really help our marketing team.' They might also ask for clarification on specific details that suggest they are visualising ownership, like 'What kind of support do you offer once we're onboarded?'

Non-verbal cues can be more subtle yet just as telling, particularly during video calls or face-to-face meetings. Is the prospect leaning in, nodding more frequently in agreement or maintaining strong eye contact? Is their tone of voice becoming more enthusiastic or positive? Are they posing fewer challenging questions and more collaborative ones? These can all suggest increasing engagement and a readiness to move forward. Conversely, if they suddenly appear distracted, begin looking at their watch or their body language becomes closed off (arms crossed, leaning back), it may indicate that you haven't fully addressed their concerns and it might not be the right moment to press for a close.

From Proposal to Commitment

Before you pursue the final close, it's often wise to test the waters with 'trial closes' throughout the sales conversation, especially after you've explained a key benefit or addressed an objection. A trial close is a low-pressure question designed to gauge the prospect's interest and see if they're aligning with you. It assists you in understanding whether you're on the right track or if there are still unresolved concerns. Examples of trial close questions include, 'Does that sound like it would address the challenge you mentioned with X? or 'Can you see how this approach might be beneficial for your team? or 'Based on what we've discussed so far, how is this sounding to you?' Their responses to these mini-questions will provide you with valuable feedback and help you determine if the main closing moment is approaching.

Once the buying signals are positive and you've successfully used a trial close to confirm their interest, it's time to select an appropriate closing technique. Remember, the aim isn't to trick anyone but to make it easy and natural for them to commit. Here are several proven techniques, particularly suited for entrepreneurs who wish to maintain trust and build long-term relationships.

1. The Assumptive Close:
This technique is used when you have strong reasons to believe the prospect is ready to buy, based on their positive signals and feedback

throughout the conversation. You proceed with the assumption that they've decided to move forward and discuss the next logical steps. For example, 'Great, so to get you started with the Pro plan, I just need to confirm the primary contact for onboarding. Would that be you or someone else on your team?'

A word of caution: this close should only be used when you have genuinely strong buying signals. If used prematurely or without sufficient positive reinforcement, it can come across as arrogant or pushy, potentially damaging rapport. However, when used correctly, it conveys confidence and can facilitate a very smooth transition for a prospect who is already sold.

2. The Summary Close (or Benefit Summary Close):
This is a powerful and highly recommended technique for founders. It involves briefly recapping the key needs the prospect has expressed and the specific benefits your solution will provide to address those needs before asking for the sale. It reinforces the value proposition in their terms. For example, 'So, just to summarise, we've discussed how your team is struggling with [Pain Point A] and how our solution can help you [Achieve Benefit A], as well as how it addresses [Pain Point B] by providing [BenefitB]. Based on this, does it make sense to move forward with getting you set up?' This close is logical, consultative and focuses entirely on the value delivered to the client, making it easier for them to say 'yes' with confidence. If in doubt, this is the option you should choose. Even if the answer you receive is not to close the deal, it often leads to you discovering other objections that you can then address before attempting to close the deal again.

3. The Choice Close (or Alternative Close):
This technique works by offering a prospect two or more viable options, where either choice results in a sale. It gives them a sense of control and makes the decision less about 'yes or no' and more about 'which one'. For a startup, this could be, 'Based on your needs, it sounds like either our Standard package or our Premium package would be a good fit. The Standard offers X, while the Premium adds Y and Z. Which of those options feels like the better starting point for you?' Or, for implementation, 'Would you prefer to aim for a start

date towards the end of this month or would the beginning of next month work better for your team?' This gently guides them towards a commitment.

4. The 'Next Steps' Close (or Process Close):
This is a very natural and low-pressure way to close. You simply outline the clear, logical next steps involved in becoming a customer, making it seem like a straightforward process. For example, 'Okay, it sounds like we have a good fit here. The next step in our process would be for me to send over the service agreement for your review. Once that's signed, we can schedule your onboarding session, which usually takes about [timeframe]. Does that process sound good to you?' This makes the commitment feel like just another item on a to-do list, reducing perceived friction.

5. The Question Close:
Sometimes, a direct but well-phrased question is the most effective way to secure commitment. After you feel you've established value and addressed concerns, you can ask a question that naturally leads to a 'yes' or a clear indication of their intent. For example, 'Based on everything we've discussed today, do you feel that our [Product/Service Name] can help your company achieve [Their Key Goal]?' If they say 'yes', a natural follow-up is, 'Excellent. Then, shall we proceed with getting the agreement drawn up?' Another approach is, 'Is there anything else you need to know before we can move forward with this?' If they say 'no', it's a clear signal to ask for the business.

6. The 'Ben Franklin' Close (or T-Account Close):
This technique is best suited for more analytical prospects who might be carefully weighing their options. You literally (or metaphorically, if on a call) draw a T-shape on a piece of paper (or a virtual whiteboard). On one side, you list the 'Reasons to Move Forward' and on the other 'Reasons to Hesitate'. As the founder, you can guide them in populating the 'Reasons to Move Forward' column by reiterating the benefits and value points discussed. Then, you ask them to articulate any remaining reasons to hesitate. Often, seeing the benefits clearly listed and having a chance to voice and then address any final

hesitations can help them reach a positive decision. The goal is to collaboratively show that the pros heavily outweigh the cons.

7. The (Ethical) Urgency Close:
This approach must be used with extreme caution and, critically, only if the urgency is genuine and transparent. Creating false scarcity or employing pressure tactics will destroy trust, which can be fatal for a startup. However, there are times when legitimate reasons exist for a prospect to act sooner rather than later. For example, 'We have a limited number of onboarding slots available for our early adopter programme this month, which includes [Specific Extra Benefit], so if you're keen to take advantage of that, it would be good to confirm by [Date].' Or 'Our current introductory pricing for this package is valid until the end of the quarter.' If you choose to use this method, be prepared to explain the reason for the urgency clearly and honestly. Never invent it.

Confident Closes That Serve the Customer

Even with the best closing techniques, you may encounter last-minute jitters or a final objection right at the point of commitment. Don't panic. This is normal. Often, it's simply a final request for reassurance or a lingering doubt that needs to be addressed. Revisit the LAER model for handling objections (Listen, Acknowledge, Explore, Respond) from Chapter Eleven. Listen carefully, understand their final concern and address it calmly and confidently. Sometimes, merely saying, 'I understand this is a significant decision and it's natural to have a few final questions. What's on your mind?' can open the door to resolve that last hurdle.

So, what happens immediately after they say 'Yes!'? First, congratulate them on making a sound decision for their business. Express your genuine enthusiasm for partnering with them. Briefly reiterate the key value they'll receive to reinforce their choice and minimise any potential buyer's remorse. Then, clearly outline the immediate next steps. 'That's fantastic news! We're thrilled to have you onboard. The very next thing that will happen is [e.g. I'll send over the agreement by the end of the day/our onboarding specialist will reach out within

24 hours to schedule your kick-off call]. In the meantime, is there anything else you need from my end right away?' This smooth transition to the next phase (which we'll cover more in Chapter Twenty: Securing the Deal: Negotiation and Contract Management) is crucial for maintaining momentum and ensuring they feel secure in their decision.

Now, what if, despite your best efforts, they say 'no' or 'not right now' at the closing stage? This can be disheartening, especially for a founder. However, how you handle this rejection is just as important as how you deal with a 'yes'. Firstly, remain professional and gracious. Thank them for their time and for considering your solution. If appropriate and they seem open to it, you can endeavour to understand the primary reason for their decision, not to argue, but for your own learning. 'I appreciate your honesty. To help us improve, would you be willing to share the main factor that led to your decision at this time?'

If it's a 'not right now' due to timing or budget, ask if it would be acceptable to stay in touch and perhaps reconnect in a few months. Keep the door open without being pushy. Every 'no' is a learning opportunity. Was there a misalignment in needs? Did a competitor offer something more compelling? Was your value proposition not clear enough for this particular prospect? Use these insights to refine your approach for the future.

As the founder, you have a unique advantage when it comes to closing deals. Your prospects know they're speaking directly to the person who created the solution, the one with the deepest knowledge and the ultimate authority (within your startup) to make things happen. Your passion is genuine, not contrived. This can be incredibly reassuring for B2B buyers who often seek a true partnership and commitment, particularly when considering a newer vendor. Don't hesitate to let that founder's conviction shine through. Your personal dedication to their success can be a compelling closing argument in itself.

It's equally important to consciously avoid any manipulative or high-pressure closing tactics you might have encountered in outdated sales training. Techniques aimed at tricking, confusing or pressuring someone into a decision are not only unethical but also extremely harmful to a startup's reputation. You are striving to build long-term, trust-based relationships with your early clients. A sale achieved through deception is likely to result in an unhappy customer, negative word-of-mouth and a drain on your support resources. Always prioritise transparency, respect and mutual benefit. The best closes are those where both you and your new client feel genuinely positive about the outcome. Your objective is to help them reach a confident 'yes', not a hesitant one.

KEY TAKEAWAYS

- The close is the outcome of value built throughout the conversation.

- Ask for the business with confidence – you're helping solve a problem.

- Create clear, easy-to-say-yes offers with defined next steps.

FOUNDER'S FIELDWORK

List Your Buying Signals: write down cues that suggest a prospect is close to buying (e.g. asking about pricing, timelines, objections).

Develop a 'Trial Close' Question Bank: draught five soft questions to test commitment (e.g. 'How would you implement this internally?').

Objection Anticipation: list the top three reasons someone might hesitate to close. Prepare one way to address each with empathy.

Create a Confidence Map: for each hot lead, rate their readiness (1–5) across budget, authority, need and timing (BANT).

Build a Closing Checklist: include proposal sent, decision-maker confirmed, Return on Investment (ROI) explained, objection addressed, next step booked.

Practise Your Ask: write and rehearse two versions of your closing question – one direct, one consultative.

Proposal Review: review your latest proposal – is it easy to understand, decision-ready and risk-reducing?

Chapter twenty

SECURING THE DEAL – NEGOTIATION AND CONTRACT MANAGEMENT

'A verbal agreement isn't worth the paper it's written on.' – Samuel Goldwyn

Finalising Agreements with Professionalism

You've navigated the emotional rollercoaster, aced the presentation and finally heard those magic words – 'Yes, let's do this!' That handshake, whether virtual or physical, feels like a monumental victory. And it is! Securing that initial agreement is a testament to your product's value and your burgeoning sales skills. But hold the champagne just a moment. While the 'close' (as we discussed in Chapter Nineteen) is a critical milestone, it's not quite the finish line. Now comes the equally important phase of formalising that agreement, often involving a final round of detailed negotiation and the slightly daunting prospect of contract management. For you, the startup founder, this isn't about getting bogged down in red tape; it's about ensuring clarity, protecting your new business and laying a solid foundation for a successful client relationship. This chapter will guide you through securing the deal with professionalism and a lean startup mindset.

Think of the verbal 'yes' as reaching the summit of a challenging climb. The view is great, but you still need to ensure your equipment is secure and that you have a clear path down. The final details of negotiation and the contract itself are that essential gear. It's tempting, especially when you're eager to get started and perhaps a little intimidated by legal documents, to rush this stage or rely on vague understandings. Resist that temptation. A little diligence here can save you a world of headaches later. Your aim is to transform that enthusiastic 'yes' into a clear, mutually understood and legally sound commitment.

Even after a prospect has verbally agreed to move forward, it's not uncommon for a few last-minute questions or minor points of negotiation to surface as you begin to discuss the specifics of the agreement. This isn't necessarily a sign of bad faith; often, it's just the client conducting their due diligence as the commitment becomes more tangible. Don't panic or feel like the deal is unravelling. This is a normal part of the process. Your role here is to remain calm, confident and anchored to the value you've already established. If the client wishes to revisit a point on pricing, scope or terms, listen carefully (Chapter Seven, always!) and understand their reasoning. Is it a genuine concern, a misunderstanding or perhaps a 'nibble' (as discussed in Chapter Nine)? Refer back to your earlier conversations and the benefits they agreed were important. 'I understand you're looking at the budget again. As we discussed, the X and Y features are designed to save your team approximately [quantifiable benefit] each month, which we calculated would offer a clear return on this investment. Is that understanding still aligned?'

This is where your preparation on your walk-away points and potential trade-offs becomes crucial. If they're asking for a small concession that doesn't fundamentally undermine the deal or your business model, you might consider it, especially if you can obtain something of value in return (like a commitment to a case study, faster payment or a longer contract term). However, be cautious about significantly altering core aspects of the deal at this late stage, as it can set a precedent or devalue your offering. As the founder, you have the authority to be flexible, but that flexibility should be strategic, not desperate. I remember once, one of my sales team made a major price concession to secure the deal with a massive USA-based retailer. That concession stayed with us forever, for years, because the first price you agree on is the one that all price increases will be based upon and judged against.

It was still a good deal; it earned us a lot of money, a lot of publicity and a foothold in the retail sector, but it could have gone badly wrong and created a legacy we could not cope with.

Before you even start drafting a formal document, take a moment to verbally reconfirm the key terms with your client. A simple email summarising the main points of your verbal agreement can be incredibly useful: 'Great speaking with you, [Client Name]! Just to recap, we agreed on [Your Product/Service Package], at a price of [Price] per [Month/Year/Project], with a start date of [Date] and the key deliverables being A, B and C. Does that accurately capture our understanding before I prepare the formal agreement?' This simple step ensures everyone is on the same page and can pre-empt misunderstandings before they get enshrined in a contract.

Contracts as Trust Builders

For an entrepreneur who has built their business on passion and perhaps a close-knit early team, the idea of introducing a formal contract, especially with your very first clients, can sometimes feel rather stiff. You might think, 'We had a great conversation, we trust each other, isn't a handshake (or a clear email chain) enough?' While trust is wonderful, a well-drafted contract isn't a sign of mistrust; it's a sign of professionalism and a tool for clarity. It protects both you and your client by clearly outlining expectations, responsibilities and what happens if things don't go as planned.

Think of your first contract not as a legal hurdle, but as a blueprint for a successful working relationship. It compels you to consider all the important details of the engagement, many of which might not have been explicitly covered in your sales conversations. What exactly are you promising to deliver? By when? What are their responsibilities? How will payment work? What happens if one party wants to end the agreement early? Having these elements written down minimises ambiguity and provides a clear reference point if questions arise later. This clarity is even more crucial when your product or service is new and potentially still evolving, as it helps manage expectations from the outset.

Furthermore, establishing the practice of using contracts from your very first deal sets a professional precedent for your business. It signals that you take your commitments seriously and expect the same from your clients. As your startup grows and you start dealing with larger clients or more complex projects, having solid contractual foundations will be indispensable. Starting this habit early, even if your first contracts are quite simple, is a smart move.

Avoiding Pitfalls and Protecting Both Parties

The thought of drafting a contract can be intimidating, conjuring images of dense legal language that only a lawyer could love. But for an early-stage startup, your first B2B contracts don't need to be (and probably shouldn't be) hundred-page behemoths. Your aim is to create a document that is clear, fair, comprehensive enough to cover the essentials and, importantly, understandable to both you and your client. Keep it as simple as the complexity of your offering allows. While every business and every deal is different, here are some key elements that a basic B2B contract for a startup should generally include:

1. Identification of Parties: clearly state the full legal names and addresses of your business and the client's business. If you are a sole proprietor, use your name.

2. Detailed Scope of Work (SOW) or Service Level Agreement (SLA): this section is the heart of the contract. Be specific about the product or service you are providing. What features, functionalities or activities are included? What are the boundaries? What is excluded? For a service, what are the specific deliverables? For software, what level of access or usage is granted? If there are service levels (e.g. uptime guarantees, support response times – though be cautious about over-promising as a startup), outline them here. The more detail you provide, the less room there will be for future disagreement.

3. Deliverables and Timelines: if there are specific deliverables (e.g. a report, a piece of custom code, product completion or the conclusion of an onboarding phase), list them clearly. Specify realistic timelines

for these deliverables. If client input or action is required for you to meet these timelines, make that clear too (e.g. 'Client to provide necessary access/materials by X date').

4. Payment Terms: clearly state the price. Is it a one-time fee, a recurring subscription (monthly, annually) or project-based? When is payment due (e.g. upfront, net 30 days, upon milestones)? What are the accepted payment methods? It is wise to include a clause regarding late payment fees or interest, though approach this tactfully.

5. Term of Agreement and Renewal: how long does the agreement last? Is it for a fixed term (e.g. 12 months)? Does it automatically renew unless one party provides notice? If so, what is the required notice period? For a startup, shorter initial terms or easier opt-outs might be more appealing to early clients but consider what would provide stability for your business.

6. Confidentiality: it is common for both parties to share confidential information during a business relationship. A mutual confidentiality clause (sometimes called a Non-Disclosure Agreement or NDA, which can also be a separate document) outlines how such information should be protected and not disclosed to third parties.

7. Intellectual Property (IP): this is particularly important if you provide creative services, developing custom software or if your solution involves your client's data. The contract should clarify who owns any pre-existing IP and who owns any IP created during the engagement. For SaaS products, you are usually granting a licence to use your IP, not transferring ownership.

8. Limitation of Liability: this is a crucial clause for protecting your startup. It seeks to limit the amount of damages your company could be liable for if something goes wrong (e.g. limiting liability to the amount paid under the contract in the last X months). While clients might push back on this, it is a standard and important way to manage your business risk, especially when you are new and have limited resources.

9. Termination Clauses: how can the agreement be concluded? Under what circumstances can either party terminate (e.g. for breach of contract, with a specific notice period, even without cause)? What occurs upon termination (e.g. final payments due, return of confidential information)?

10. Governing Law and Dispute Resolution: specify which jurisdiction's laws will govern the contract (usually your state or country). It's also advisable to include a clause about how disputes will be managed, perhaps commencing with informal negotiation or mediation before resorting to more formal legal action. For a startup, keeping this straightforward is recommended.

Strive to use plain English wherever possible. While certain legal terms are unavoidable, the overall document should be comprehensible to a non-lawyer. If you don't understand a clause, how can you expect your client to? This transparency fosters trust.

So, where do you obtain this essential document, especially when you're bootstrapping? You don't necessarily need to spend thousands on a lawyer to draft your very first simple contract.

There are numerous reputable online sources for contract templates and industry-specific associations sometimes provide samples. If you use a template, ensure it's tailored for your jurisdiction and B2B agreements. Read it very carefully and customise it thoroughly to suit your specific offering and the particulars of the deal. A generic template used indiscriminately is nearly worse than having no contract at all. Caveat emptor applies strongly here; ensure the source is credible, particularly if you choose to use one of the many large language model (LLM) AI-based systems such as Gemini or ChatGPT to draft your contract.

However, there will come a point, possibly even with your first few significant deals, when a generic template simply isn't sufficient, or when the client wishes to utilise their much more complex contract. This is where seeking affordable legal advice becomes a wise investment rather than an expense. Don't assume that you need a high-priced corporate law firm. Look for the following:

Lawyers specialising in startups or small businesses: they understand common challenges and can often provide more tailored, cost-effective advice.

Fixed-fee services: many lawyers now offer fixed fees for reviewing or drafting standard contracts, which helps you to budget.

Legal tech platforms: some platforms connect you with lawyers for specific tasks at more accessible rates.

University legal clinics or pro bono programmes: if your startup has a social mission or you meet certain criteria, these can sometimes be an option.

Even if you seek legal assistance, your responsibility as the founder is to fully understand what you're signing and what you're asking your client to sign. Don't simply outsource and forget it; ask your lawyer to explain any clauses you don't understand. This knowledge will empower you in future negotiations.

Once your contract is drafted (and ideally reviewed, if necessary), don't simply email it as an attachment with a one-liner: 'Here's the contract, please sign.' This can feel impersonal and might lead to your client immediately becoming defensive or getting bogged down in the legalese. Instead, treat the presentation of the contract as another opportunity to reinforce the value of your partnership and ensure clarity.

Consider scheduling a brief call to walk them through the key sections. You're not giving legal advice but you can explain the intent behind the main clauses in plain language. 'I've sent over the agreement and I just wanted to quickly highlight a few key areas: Section 3 outlines the scope of services that we discussed, Section 5 covers the payment schedule and Section 8 is our standard confidentiality clause to protect both our interests. Please take your time to review it and I'm here to answer any questions you might have about how it reflects our conversation.'

This proactive approach demonstrates professionalism and can pre-empt many questions or concerns. It also makes you appear open and transparent, which builds trust. Be prepared for them to have questions or to request reasonable modifications. Not every client will sign your standard agreement without a single change. Listen to their requests, understand their rationale and decide if the requested changes are acceptable to your business. This is a mini-negotiation in itself. Know your non-negotiables but be open to minor, sensible adjustments that don't compromise your core interests.

Once you and your client are happy with the terms, it's time to get it signed. The days of printing, signing, scanning and emailing back and forth are largely over, thankfully. Electronic signature (e-signature) tools have made this process incredibly simple, efficient and legally binding in most jurisdictions for most types of agreements. Many e-signature platforms offer free or very affordable tiers that are perfect for startups. Tools like:

HelloSign (now Dropbox Sign)

DocuSign (has eSignature for individual or very small business options)

Adobe Acrobat Reader DC (often has a free 'Fill & Sign' feature for basic needs, though dedicated e-sign platforms offer more robust tracking)

PandaDoc (offers a free eSign plan)

These tools allow you to upload your document, specify where signatures and dates are required, send it securely to your client and receive notifications when it is viewed and signed. They also provide an audit trail, which enhances legal validity. Ensure that all parties needing to sign (both on your side and the client's) do so accurately.

The moment that signed contract arrives back in your inbox is certainly cause for a small celebration! You've officially secured the deal. However, your work isn't quite finished. A few final steps will ensure a smooth transition from 'deal closed' to 'happy, successful client'.

First, thank your new client enthusiastically for their business and reaffirm your excitement about the partnership. 'Fantastic news, [Client Name]! We've received the signed agreement and are absolutely thrilled to officially welcome [Their Company] as a client. We're really looking forward to helping you achieve [Key Outcome].'

Securely store the signed contract. Whether it's in a dedicated cloud folder, your CRM or a specific contract management system (if you eventually use one), ensure you have an organised, easily accessible and backed-up repository for all your signed agreements. You'll need to refer to it. Most importantly, clearly communicate the immediate next steps for onboarding or service commencement. Don't leave them wondering what happens next. 'Our onboarding specialist, [Name], will be reaching out to you within the next 24 hours to schedule your kick-off call and get you set up with [Your Product/Service]. In the meantime, if you have any initial questions, please don't hesitate to ask.' (Chapter Twenty-One will delve into Building Long-Term Client Relationships and Chapter Twenty-Two into Customer Success Management and Retention, both of which commence from this point).

This final stage of securing the deal, from finalising the last negotiation points to managing the contract process, may not be the most glamorous part of sales, but it is where a promising verbal agreement transforms into a solid business commitment. As a founder, managing this with diligence, transparency and a focus on mutual understanding will not only protect your startup but also cultivate the kind of trust that turns your first clients into long-term partners.

KEY TAKEAWAYS

- Professional contracts protect both parties and build trust.

- A good agreement outlines deliverables, scope, pricing and expectations clearly.

- Secure deals swiftly and cleanly – delays create doubt.

FOUNDER'S FIELDWORK

Review a Simple Contract Template: familiarise yourself with key sections like scope, payment terms and IP. Flag areas you'd negotiate.

Draft Your Own Deal Summary Email: include terms, timing and a friendly nudge. Use this as your standard send post-verbal agreement and before a contract.

Role-Play a Price Pushback: have someone challenge your pricing. Practise justifying value without discounting first.

Define Your Redlines: write your top three non-negotiables for contracts (e.g. payment terms, usage rights, termination clauses).

Create a 'Soft Exit' Option: offer prospects a flexible clause or trial that reduces risk and speeds up deal closure.

Close Loop Audit: track the average time from verbal yes to signed contract. Aim to reduce lag and improve process clarity.

Chapter twenty-one

BUILDING LONG-TERM CLIENT RELATIONSHIPS

'Make a customer, not a sale.' – Katherine Barchetti

Beyond the Close – Delivering on Your Promise
You've navigated the choppy waters of the initial sale, secured the deal with a signed contract and experienced that incredible surge of accomplishment that comes with landing a new B2B client for your startup. It's a milestone worthy of celebration, no doubt. However, as the founder – and likely the first salesperson – your work doesn't stop once the ink dries. In fact, in many ways, it's just beginning. That first 'yes' is the gateway to something potentially far more valuable than a single transaction: a long-term client relationship. This chapter is about how you, the entrepreneurial salesperson, can lay the crucial foundations for these enduring partnerships, turning your first few hard-won clients into loyal advocates and a source of sustainable growth.

For a fledgling B2B business, your early clients are not just names on an invoice; they are the bedrock of your future. The lifetime value (LTV) of a happy, long-term client far exceeds the effort of continuously chasing new ones. They provide predictable revenue, invaluable feedback for your evolving product or service, compelling case studies and, if treated well, a stream of warm referrals. As a founder, your direct involvement in nurturing these initial relationships is a unique advantage. You can offer a level of personal attention, responsiveness and strategic insight that larger, more impersonal organisations often cannot match. This chapter focuses on the practical steps to build and nurture these connections from the moment the deal is signed, setting the stage for lasting loyalty.

The period immediately following the contract signing is often referred to as the 'honeymoon period' and it represents a golden opportunity to solidify the positive impression you made during the sales process. This is where you demonstrate that your startup is not just about making promises but about delivering on them. A seamless transition from the 'sales' conversation to the 'onboarding' or 'service delivery' phase is critical, even if, as the founder, you're still wearing both hats. The client shouldn't feel as though they've been passed from one department to another, especially if you are both departments. Maintain consistency in communication and ensure that all the details discussed during the sales process are clearly understood and acted upon.

Setting crystal-clear expectations from day one (post-contract) is paramount. Reconfirm the timelines, deliverables and what you'll need from them to ensure a smooth start. This is where you translate the contractual agreements into a practical working reality. Your ability to fulfil these initial promises – whether it's a swift onboarding, a perfectly configured product or the timely commencement of a service – serves as the first major test of the relationship. Meeting, or even better, exceeding these early expectations builds immense trust and reinforces their decision to choose your new company. A warm, personalised welcome that goes beyond an automated email can also make a significant difference. A quick personal call or video message from you, the founder, can make them feel truly valued.

Consistent, proactive communication forms the lifeline of any healthy client relationship. As a startup, you cannot afford for your early clients to feel ignored or as though they are shouting into a void. Your communication should transcend purely transactional updates (like 'your report is ready') and foster relational interactions. Schedule regular, brief check-ins, particularly in the early months. The frequency will depend on the nature of your offering but a quick call or a personalised email every few weeks to gauge their progress, address any questions or share a relevant insight can be immensely beneficial. Don't wait for them to approach you with problems; proactively seek their feedback.

Being accessible, within reasonable boundaries, is a significant advantage you possess as a founder. While you cannot be on call 24/7, informing your early key clients that they have a direct line to you for important issues can be incredibly reassuring. This doesn't mean you become their primary support channel for every minor query (you will need to establish processes for that as you grow) but for strategic concerns or urgent problems, your direct involvement demonstrates commitment.

Beyond updates about your product, consider sharing relevant industry news, insightful articles or trends that might benefit their business. This positions you as a thoughtful partner, rather than just a vendor. Delivering value consistently extends beyond simply ensuring your product or service functions as advertised. It involves continuously seeking ways to support your client's success. As your relationship develops, remain attuned to their evolving needs. Are they encountering new challenges? Are their business goals changing? Your comprehensive understanding of your offering, combined with your insights into their business, might enable you to identify opportunities to provide additional value. These could manifest through offering strategic advice based on your expertise, connecting them with other useful contacts in your network or perhaps even suggesting small enhancements or add-ons to your service (if feasible and genuinely beneficial for them) that they hadn't previously considered.

Turn Clients into Advocates

The goal is to ensure they feel like a truly valued partner, not merely a line item on your revenue forecast. One of the most effective ways to ascertain that they are receiving value, particularly with a new or evolving product, is to establish robust early feedback loops. Encourage them to share their experiences – what's working well, what's frustrating, what features they wish they had. This not only aids you in refining your offering but also makes them feel heard and invested in your mutual success. This kind of dialogue is fundamental to building a partnership that endures beyond the initial contract term.

As the founder, you possess a unique opportunity to transcend the typical vendor-client dynamic and become a trusted advisor. Your expertise extends beyond your specific product; it likely encompasses the broader problem domain your startup addresses. Don't hesitate to leverage this. When you comprehend their business goals, you can provide strategic insights that surpass the immediate scope of your service. Perhaps you identify an opportunity for them to utilise your solution in a new way to achieve a competitive advantage, or you might share lessons learned from other (anonymised) interactions in the market. This fosters incredible loyalty.

This advisory role also arises from taking a genuine, proactive interest in their business success. Celebrate their wins with them. Understand their pressures. The more they perceive you as someone who 'gets' their world and is actively rooting for them, the stronger the bond becomes. Building personal rapport with key contacts within their organisation is equally important. People buy from people and they continue to do business with those they like and trust. Remembering small personal details, grasping their communication preferences and simply being a pleasant, professional person to deal with can make a surprising difference.

Even with the best intentions and the most diligent efforts, early bumps in the road are almost inevitable when you're a startup. Your product might harbour an unexpected bug, a service delivery could hit a snag or there may simply have been a miscommunication. How you navigate these challenges truly tests the relationship and presents a massive opportunity to build (or break) trust.

Do not shy away from problems. If something goes awry on your end, acknowledge it quickly and transparently. Recognise the issue, apologise sincerely for any inconvenience caused and clearly convey what you're doing to rectify it and prevent a recurrence.

Your direct involvement as the founder in troubleshooting and demonstrating a commitment to rapid resolution can transform a potentially negative situation into a powerful display of your company's responsiveness. Clients recognise that new businesses are learning and that perfection is elusive. What they value is honesty, effort and a clear commitment to making things right. Proactively communicating about any known issues that might affect them before they discover them also builds significant trust. It shows respect for their operations and allows them to plan accordingly. When I was a buyer with Mars Incorporated, a logistics supplier let me down badly but before I found this out, they were speaking to me on the phone. They explained what had gone wrong, why it had happened, what they had done to try and negate the problem and prevent it from occurring again and, of course, apologised. Compare that to another former supplier I had there who messed up and attempted to shift the blame to our team. The truth was easy to uncover and both were start-up businesses; needless to say, the first company became a preferred supplier.

Ongoing Communication, not Just Check-Ins

As your clients begin to achieve successes, partly through the use of your product or service, make a point of acknowledging and celebrating those wins with them. This could be as simple as a congratulatory email or a quick mention in a check-in call. 'I saw your team hit that important Q3 target – fantastic news! We're thrilled that our platform could play a small part in helping you streamline the process.' This shows you're paying attention and are invested in their outcomes. It also subtly reinforces the value you're delivering. These moments of shared success are also natural opportunities to gather positive feedback or even ask if they'd be willing to provide a testimonial or act as a reference down the line, once the value is clearly established. Never underestimate the simple power of saying 'thank you', beyond the automated acknowledgement of an invoice payment. Especially with your first few clients, who are taking a chance on your new venture, small gestures of appreciation can significantly contribute to building goodwill. This doesn't necessarily mean expensive gifts. It could be a handwritten note after a particularly successful phase of a project, a small piece of company swag (if you have any) or simply taking a few extra minutes in conversation to express your genuine gratitude for their business and partnership. Making them feel like a truly valued and foundational client fosters a sense of loyalty that's hard to replicate.

As your relationship with these early clients matures and as your own startup's offerings potentially expand, you can start to think about laying the groundwork for future growth with them. This isn't about aggressive upselling; it's about naturally identifying opportunities where they could benefit from using more of your services or new features as their own business evolves or as you release new capabilities. Because you've built trust and understand their needs deeply, these conversations can feel like a natural extension of your advisory role. 'As your team grows, you might find our enhanced reporting module useful for X reason – it's something we've developed based on feedback from clients like you.'

Furthermore, by delivering exceptional early experiences and consistently providing value, you create your most powerful sales and marketing assets: delighted customers who are willing to become advocates. Encourage this advocacy. Once you've delivered clear results, don't be shy about asking if they'd be comfortable providing a testimonial, participating in a case study or making an introduction to another company in their network that might also benefit from your solution. A referral from a happy client is sales gold; it comes with pre-built trust and credibility.

There will come a point, hopefully, when your startup has grown beyond just you and a handful of initial clients. As you onboard more customers and perhaps even start to build a dedicated customer success or account management function (as we'll discuss in Chapter Twenty-Two), the challenge becomes how to scale the kind of personalised relationship-building that you, the founder, initially provided. While processes and systems will become necessary, it's crucial to ensure that the empathetic, value-driven, founder-led ethos that built those first strong relationships isn't lost in translation. The principles you apply in nurturing your very first clients – deep listening, proactive communication, consistent value delivery and genuine partnership – should become ingrained in your company's DNA. This must be part of the onboarding for every new hire you bring into your company as you grow; it is part of your culture.

Building long-term client relationships is an ongoing commitment, not a one-off project. It necessitates consistent effort, genuine care and a relentless focus on helping your clients achieve their goals. For an entrepreneur, these early relationships are more than mere revenue streams; they are your learning ground, your source of credibility and the foundation upon which you will build a sustainable and successful B2B business.

KEY TAKEAWAYS

- Client retention is more valuable than acquisition – don't disappear after the deal.

- Over-deliver on value and stay engaged to drive upsells and referrals.

- Strong relationships become your best marketing engine.

FOUNDER'S FIELDWORK

Client Success Plan: for each new customer, map out their desired outcome and how you'll help them achieve it.

Schedule a Thirty-Day Check-In Call: for every new client, book a follow-up conversation to review early outcomes and feedback.

Create a 'Customer Success Touchpoint Plan': map out how often and how you'll stay in touch, e.g. monthly calls, quarterly reviews.

Send a Surprise Value Email: share a useful article, insight or intro with a client, unprompted. Build goodwill without selling.

Ask for a Quick Testimonial: after a client win, request one sentence of praise you can use in future marketing.

Track Client Relationship Health: create a simple system (green/yellow/red) to evaluate how each client feels about your service.

PART 5

SCALING WHAT WORKS

Now that you've established a foundation, it's time to scale. In this final section, you'll discover how to retain customers, measure what matters, stay ahead of the market and eventually transition from founder-led selling to building a team. It's about transforming your sales hustle into a repeatable system.

Chapter twenty-two

CUSTOMER SUCCESS MANAGEMENT AND RETENTION

'Customer service shouldn't just be a department; it should be the entire company.' – Tony Hsieh

Customer Success Begins at Onboarding

The ink is dry on the contract, the virtual handshake has been exchanged and you've just secured another crucial B2B client for your fledgling startup. That feeling of triumph is well-deserved. You've successfully navigated the sales process and convinced someone to believe in your vision and offering. However, if you think the sales journey ends there, you're missing the biggest opportunity of all. That initial sale is merely the prologue; the main story, which truly determines your startup's long-term viability, revolves around what happens after the deal is signed. Welcome to the world of Customer Success Management (CSM) and retention – the art and science of ensuring your clients achieve their desired outcomes, remain with you for the long haul and become advocates for your business.

For an entrepreneur just starting out, Customer Success Management might sound like a fancy corporate term, something reserved for companies with dedicated departments and sophisticated software. Let's strip away that mystique. In its simplest, most startup-friendly form, CSM is the proactive effort you make to ensure your customers successfully utilise your product or service to achieve their goals. It's about making their success your business. And why is this so critical? Because in the B2B world, acquiring a new customer is often five to twenty-five times more expensive than retaining an existing one. Your early customers are your lifeblood. If they churn out as quickly as you bring them in, you're on a treadmill to nowhere. Retained customers, on the other hand, provide predictable revenue, invaluable feedback, become less price-sensitive over time and are often your best source of referrals and glowing testimonials. For a lean startup, a strong focus on retention through CSM isn't a luxury; it's a core survival and growth strategy.

As the founder, you are, by default, your company's first Customer Success Manager. Frankly, in these early days, no one is better suited for the role. You possess the deepest understanding of your product's vision, an unparalleled passion for solving the customer's problem and the authority to quickly address issues or adapt to feedback. Your direct involvement signals to these crucial early clients that their success is a top priority for the entire company, right from the very top. This personal touch is a powerful differentiator.

Proactive Success, not Reactive Support

It's important to distinguish Customer Success Management from traditional customer service. Customer service is typically reactive – when a client has a problem, they contact you and you assist them in fixing it. That's essential, of course. But CSM is proactive. It's about anticipating your customers' needs, guiding them towards best practices, ensuring they're extracting the full value from your offering and helping them achieve their specific business outcomes before they encounter major roadblocks or feel the need to complain. You're not just solving problems; you're engineering success. This proactive approach is particularly vital when your product is new or innovative, as clients may not instinctively know how to maximise its potential. Your role is to be their guide and trusted advisor on that journey.

The period immediately following the sale, often the first ninety days, is absolutely critical in setting the stage for long-term retention. This is where effective onboarding becomes your first and most important CSM activity. Onboarding is far more than merely getting them technically set up or providing them with a login for a system, if that's what you sell. It is about ensuring they understand how your product or service will assist them in achieving the specific goals they discussed during the sales process. It's about creating a smooth transition and fulfilling those initial promises. One of your primary aims during onboarding should be to help your new client achieve a 'quick win' – an early, tangible piece of value they obtain from your solution. This builds their confidence, reinforces their decision to choose you and generates positive momentum.

To achieve this, you need to collaborate with them to define what success actually looks like. What were their desired outcomes when they signed up? Was it to save a specific amount of time, increase a particular metric, streamline a specific process or resolve a nagging operational headache? Don't presume you know. Inquire with them. Document these goals, even if it's simply in your straightforward CRM or spreadsheet notes for that client. Then, customise your onboarding and early interactions to assist them in achieving those specific outcomes. Regularly revisiting these goals with them ensures you're both aligned and allows you to demonstrate the value they're receiving over time.

Once they're onboarded, your founder-led CSM efforts transition to proactive engagement and ongoing value reinforcement. This doesn't mean pestering them. It means having purposeful check-ins. Schedule brief calls or send personalised emails at sensible intervals. The aim isn't merely to ask, 'How's it going?' Instead, come prepared. You might share a new tip or best practice for using your product, point them to a new feature that might be particularly relevant to a goal they mentioned or offer insights based on how other (anonymised) clients in similar situations are achieving success. Your goal is to continuously remind them, subtly or directly, of the value they are receiving and to help them uncover even more.

Think of yourself as an extension of their team, albeit an external one. The more you understand their business context, industry and specific operational challenges, the more valuable your advice becomes. This is where your founder's perspective can be incredibly powerful. You didn't merely build a product; you likely possess profound insights into the problem space. Share those insights. Sometimes, the most valuable CSM interaction isn't about your product at all but about offering a piece of strategic advice or a connection that assists their broader business. This elevates your relationship beyond a simple vendor-client dynamic.

As always, listening remains paramount, particularly in the context of Customer Success Management (CSM). Every interaction presents an opportunity to gather feedback. How are customers finding the product? What is working well? What are their current frustrations or unmet needs? This feedback is invaluable, not just for refining your product roadmap, but for identifying potential issues that could lead to churn if left unaddressed. It also helps you understand if their desired outcomes are evolving, allowing you to adjust your support accordingly.

In the early days, you do not need sophisticated dashboards and complex algorithms to monitor customer health. Simple observation and attentive listening can reveal a great deal. If your product is software, are customers actively using it? Are key features being adopted? A sudden drop-off in usage can be a red flag. How frequent and how positive is your communication with them? If a previously engaged client suddenly goes silent or their tone becomes consistently negative, it is worth investigating. Are they achieving the milestones they set out to accomplish with your solution? If not, why not? A proactive conversation can often set things back on track.

When you receive feedback, whether it is a suggestion for improvement or a complaint, how you handle it is crucial for retention. Make your clients feel heard. Acknowledge their input promptly and express gratitude, even if it is critical. Where appropriate, explain how you are addressing their concerns or incorporating their feedback. Even if you cannot implement every suggestion immediately (which is often the case for a resource-constrained startup), closing the loop and demonstrating that their voice matters builds immense loyalty. When you do make an improvement based on client feedback, be sure to inform them! 'Remember that suggestion you had about X? We've just implemented it!' This approach makes them feel like valued partners in your development.

Measuring, Managing and Retaining

Despite your best efforts, some customers will inevitably become 'at-risk'. Identifying these situations early is key. Common warning signs include decreased usage, a string of unresolved (or poorly resolved) support issues, a change in their key contact who was your internal champion, an expressed interest in competitor solutions, or just a general negative sentiment in your interactions. For your crucial early clients, it might be worthwhile creating a simple mental (or written) 'at-risk checklist'.

When you identify an at-risk client, don't bury your head in the sand. Proactive intervention is your best approach. Reach out and seek to understand the core reasons for their dissatisfaction or disengagement. Is it a product issue? A misunderstanding of value? A change in their business needs? Once you grasp the problem, collaborate with them to find a solution. This might involve providing additional training, assisting them in reconfiguring your solution to better meet their needs, or, in some cases, offering a concession such as a temporary discount or an added-value service if it aligns with your business and can genuinely salvage the relationship.

Sometimes, even with your most heroic efforts, a client will decide to leave. Churn is a painful reality for any business, particularly a startup. When it occurs, endeavour to conduct a (gentle and respectful) exit interview or send a brief survey.

Understanding the primary reasons for their departure is invaluable. Was it price? A missing feature? Poor service? A change in their own business strategy? Analyse this feedback for patterns. Every lost customer, while disappointing, is a lesson that can help you refine your product, pricing, sales process, or CSM approach to mitigate future churn. It's also vital to recognise that not every customer is a suitable fit indefinitely. Sometimes, a client outgrows your solution, or their needs diverge so significantly that parting ways is the natural and optimal outcome for both parties.

Beyond these structured CSM activities, there are numerous low-cost, high-impact tactics that you, as the founder, can employ to enhance retention. The importance of a personal touch cannot be overstated. A handwritten thank-you note after a significant milestone, an email sharing an article you genuinely believe would interest them (with no sales pitch attached), or recalling a small personal detail from a previous conversation can make a client feel uniquely valued. For certain types of products, you might even consider creating a small, informal community for your early users – perhaps a private LinkedIn group, a Slack channel, or a WhatsApp group where they can share tips, ask questions and learn from each other (and from you). This fosters a sense of belonging and shared purpose. Simple loyalty gestures, such as acknowledging their anniversary as a client or offering them early, exclusive access to new features you're developing, can also go a long way.

Ultimately, the goal of your founder-led Customer Success Management is to turn your satisfied clients into your most powerful marketing assets: enthusiastic advocates. When a client is genuinely succeeding with your solution and feels valued by your company, they are far more likely to provide glowing testimonials, agree to be featured in a case study or, most importantly, to refer new business to you. Don't hesitate to ask for these things but do so at the right moment – after they've clearly experienced and acknowledged the value you provide.

Make it easy for them to advocate. Provide them with a simple template for a testimonial or offer to draft the case study for their approval. A warm referral from a trusted peer is the holy grail of leads. As your startup grows, you'll eventually need to consider how to scale your CSM efforts. The deeply personal involvement you had with your first ten clients might not be feasible with your first hundred. This doesn't mean abandoning the principles, but rather thinking about how to incorporate them into more structured processes or, eventually, dedicated roles.

Even if it's still just you, you might start by allocating specific blocks of time each week solely for proactive CSM activities. Documenting what worked well with your early clients – the check-in cadences, the common questions, the successful onboarding steps – will be invaluable when you eventually bring someone else in to help manage customer success. The ethos you establish as the founder, focused on genuine partnership and proactive value delivery, should become the guiding philosophy for all future customer-facing interactions. Your legacy in CSM is built from these very first relationships.

KEY TAKEAWAYS

- Customer success drives retention, expansion and referrals – it's revenue protection.

- Onboarding or delivery is a critical moment to prove your value and build loyalty.

- Proactivity and clear communication keep customers engaged and satisfied.

FOUNDER'S FIELDWORK

Define Success Metrics for Each Client: identify how each client defines success (e.g. time saved, ROI) and align your support accordingly.

Create a Basic Success Dashboard: track usage, feedback, support issues and account status for each client in a spreadsheet or CRM.

Design a Customer Onboarding Checklist: ensure you deliver a consistent value-focused first experience to every new customer.

Review Your Churn Risks: list any clients at risk of leaving and define one action per account to proactively improve retention.

Send a Quarterly Health Survey: ask three questions on satisfaction, desired improvements and the likelihood to refer. Track trends over time.

Chapter twenty-three

MEASURING AND ANALYSING SALES PERFORMANCE

'What gets measured gets managed.' – Peter Drucker

Sales is a System, not a Mystery

You're in the thick of it. You're the founder, the product visionary, the chief marketer and, as we've been exploring, the primary salesperson. You're having conversations, sending emails and perhaps even delivering a few demos. But how do you actually know if what you're doing is working? Or, more importantly, how do you figure out what's not working so you can fix it quickly, before you burn through your precious time and energy?

This is where measuring and analysing your sales performance comes in. Now, before you picture complex dashboards and impenetrable spreadsheets filled with acronyms, let's be clear: for an entrepreneur just starting up, this isn't about drowning in data. It's about tracking a few vital signs for your sales efforts, using simple tools, so you can make smart, informed decisions on the fly.

Many founders, especially when they're the sole salesperson, fall into the trap of thinking, 'I'm too busy actually selling (and building the product and everything else!) to spend time measuring things.' Or 'I only have a handful of prospects, what's there to measure?' This is a dangerous mindset for a lean startup. In these early days, every interaction, every response (or lack thereof), every tiny win and every setback is a piece of crucial data.

You're operating with limited resources, so understanding which of your sales activities are effective and which are just spinning your wheels is paramount. Measurement is how you learn. It's how you iterate on your sales approach, just as you iterate on your product. It's the compass that tells you if you're heading in the right direction or if you need to adjust your course. Without it, you're essentially flying blind, relying on gut feel alone, which can be notoriously unreliable when you're so close to your own creation.

The Metrics That Matter

So, what should a busy founder actually track? The key is to keep it simple, actionable and focused on metrics that give you real insight. Don't attempt to measure everything; that leads to 'analysis paralysis'. Instead, focus on a handful of key performance indicators (KPIs) that reflect the health and effectiveness of your sales activities. It's often useful to think about these in two categories:

Leading indicators (which track your sales activities) and lagging indicators (which monitor the outcomes of those activities) are important to consider. Early on, when results may be sporadic, your activity metrics tend to be more revealing and easier to manage.

Let's examine some Key Activity Metrics (Inputs) that merit your attention:

Number of Outreach Attempts: this is a straightforward count of the emails you send, the LinkedIn messages you dispatch, or the calls you make (if cold calling is part of your strategy). Tracking this helps you understand the sheer volume of effort you're investing at the very top of your sales funnel.

Number of Meaningful Conversations/First Meetings Booked: an outreach attempt is one thing; obtaining a substantive response that leads to a scheduled conversation, or an initial meeting, is another. This metric indicates whether your initial messaging is resonating sufficiently to earn some of your prospect's valuable time.

Number of Demos or Presentations Delivered: if your sales process involves a product demonstration or a more formal presentation of your solution, tracking how many of these you conduct is essential. It's a pivotal milestone in advancing a prospect.

Number of Proposals Sent (if applicable to your sales model): if you typically send a formal proposal or quote after a demonstration or detailed discussion, monitoring this number is significant. It represents prospects who have progressed to a more serious stage of consideration.

These activity metrics are largely within your control. You can choose to send more emails or make more calls. They indicate the effort aspect of the equation.

Next are the Key Outcome Metrics (Outputs). These monitor the results of your efforts. Initially, these numbers will likely be small, but it's essential to begin tracking them from day one:

Number of New Leads Generated (from specific activities): where are your conversations arising? If you're experimenting with different outreach methods, which ones are actually producing individuals who enter your sales process? (This connects back to Chapter Thirteen on Lead Generation.)

Conversion Rates at Each Stage: this is where things become really insightful. You're examining the percentage of prospects who progress from one stage of your sales process to the next. For instance: outreach attempts to meaningful conversations (e.g. if 100 emails yield five meetings, that's a 5% conversion rate).

Meaningful conversations to demos delivered.

Demos delivered to proposals sent.

Proposals sent to deals closed (won).

Number of New Clients Won: the ultimate lagging indicator! This is the reward.

Average Deal Size (if applicable): if your pricing varies, what's the typical value of a new client? This will become more relevant as you secure a few deals.

Sales Cycle Length: how long does it generally take from your first contact with a prospect to the day they sign on the dotted line? Understanding this aids you in predicting future revenue (however roughly) and managing your own expectations.

The beauty of being a lean startup is that you don't need sophisticated, expensive software to track these vital signs. Your 'Founder's Sales Dashboard' can be remarkably low-tech but highly effective.

A spreadsheet (like Google Sheets or Microsoft Excel) is often the perfect starting point. You can create a simple sheet to log your activities. For instance, columns could include:

Prospect Name, Company, Contact Date, Outreach Method (Email 1, LinkedIn Message, Call), Response Received (Yes/No/Type), Date of Meeting Booked, Date of Demo, Date Proposal Sent, Date Closed (Won/Lost), Deal Value and Notes.

You can then use basic formulas to calculate your conversion rates or tally your activities.

The key is consistency in data entry. Devote just 10–15 minutes at the end of each day or week to update your records. It might feel like a chore initially but the insights you'll gain will be well worth the effort.

If you're ready for something a bit more structured than a spreadsheet, many Customer Relationship Management (CRM) systems offer free tiers that are more than sufficient for a solo founder. We touched on this in Chapter Thirteen. Tools like HubSpot CRM, Zoho CRM, or Freshsales often allow you to track contacts, log interactions (some can even sync with your email) and manage a visual sales pipeline. Some free CRMs also feature basic reporting capabilities that can automatically calculate some of your key metrics, saving you manual effort. Investing a few hours to set up and learn a free CRM can yield significant dividends in organisation and insight.

Project management tools like Trello or Asana can also be repurposed as simple visual sales pipeline trackers. You can create columns for each stage of your sales process (e.g. 'New Lead', 'Initial Contact Made', 'Meeting Scheduled', 'Demo Completed', 'Proposal Sent', 'Closed-Won', 'Closed-Lost') and move prospect 'cards' across these columns. This provides a clear visual overview of where everyone is in your funnel.

The specific tool isn't as important as the habit of consistently capturing the data. Remember the old adage: 'garbage in, garbage out'. If your data entry is sporadic or inaccurate, your analysis will be equally flawed.

From Analysis to Action
So, you've started tracking a few key numbers. Now what? How do you make sense of them in a way that actually helps you sell better? This isn't about advanced statistical analysis; it's about identifying trends and asking 'why?'.

Begin by examining trends over time. Even if it's just week-over-week or month-over-month, are your activity levels increasing? Are your conversion rates improving, remaining flat or declining? For example, if you sent 50 outreach emails last month and got two meetings and this month you sent 100 emails but still only got two meetings, that indicates something important; simply increasing volume isn't improving your results, you probably need to reassess the quality or targeting of your outreach.

Calculating simple conversion rates is where you'll find some of your most actionable insights.

If your outreach-to-meeting conversion rate is very low, it might suggest that your initial messaging isn't compelling, your targeting is off or your subject lines aren't effective in getting emails opened.

If you're securing plenty of first meetings but very few are advancing to a demo or a deeper discussion, perhaps your qualification during that first meeting isn't effective, or you're not successfully communicating your value proposition early on.

If demos are going well but few lead to proposals, are you demonstrating the appropriate features, or are prospects getting hindered by price or unvoiced objections at this stage?

If many proposals are sent but few lead to closures, this indicates potential issues with your closing skills (Chapter Nineteen), your final negotiation (Chapter Twenty), the terms of your proposal, or perhaps the prospect wasn't as qualified as you initially thought.

Identifying where the most significant drop-offs occur in your sales funnel is crucial. Your sales funnel is simply a visualisation of how prospects navigate these stages. If you start with 100 leads at the top and only two of them convert to customers, where did the other 98 go? Pinpointing the weakest areas of your funnel reveals where to concentrate your improvement efforts.

Make an effort to understand your most effective lead sources or outreach methods. When you successfully close a deal, make a note of how that relationship originated. Was it a referral? A response to a specific type of cold email? An interaction on LinkedIn? Over time, even with small numbers, patterns may emerge that indicate where your highest-quality prospects are coming from. This enables you to focus on strategies that work.

Understanding your average sales cycle length is also enlightening. If you discover it typically takes, say, 60 days from first contact to a signed deal, that helps you set realistic expectations for yourself and for future revenue projections (regardless of how basic those might be initially). It also aids in identifying if a particular deal is getting 'stuck' longer than usual.

The real power of measuring your sales performance emerges when you leverage that data to iterate and improve. This embodies the lean sales loop in action: Measure – > Analyse – > Learn – > Act – > Measure again. Your performance data isn't merely a report card; it's a diagnostic tool.

If your data indicates that outreach to specific job titles within your ICP has a much higher response rate, you can refine your targeting (Chapter Five) to concentrate more on those roles.

If you experiment with two different email subject lines for your cold outreach (Chapter Seventeen) and one consistently achieves double the open rate, you've gleaned valuable insights about your messaging.

If you notice that prospects who receive a particular piece of follow-up content are more likely to agree to a demo, that informs your content strategy (Chapter Sixteen).

If you observe that objections regarding a specific feature keep derailing demos, that's crucial feedback for your product development and for how you handle objections (Chapter Eleven).

Don't be afraid to experiment. Sales, particularly in a startup, is not a perfectly defined science. Try changing one variable in your approach – your email copy, your demo structure, your follow-up cadence – and observe what impact it has on your key metrics. Small, incremental improvements can accumulate significantly over time. Be patient and work methodically.

It's also crucial to remember that not everything that matters can be measured, especially in the early days. While quantitative metrics are vital, don't overlook qualitative feedback. This is data too, providing the 'why' behind the numbers. When you lose a deal, if the prospect is amenable, strive to understand their reasoning. Was it price? A competitor? A missing feature? A lack of trust? This direct feedback is invaluable. Maintain a simple log of common objections you encounter. What themes are emerging? What does this tell you about how your offering is perceived or where the gaps lie? Conversely, what positive feedback are you receiving? Which aspects of your product or sales approach do your new clients particularly praise? This helps you understand your strengths and what you should continue to emphasise. This qualitative data, gathered from your direct interactions as the founder, provides richness and context that numbers alone cannot offer.

What if, despite your best efforts and careful analysis, the numbers just aren't looking good? If your activity levels are high but your conversion rates are stubbornly low across the board, or if you're simply not closing any deals, this acts as your early warning system. It might indicate a problem that goes deeper than just your sales technique. Perhaps there's a fundamental misalignment between your product and the market's needs (product-market fit). Maybe your chosen ICP isn't actually experiencing the pain point you thought they were, or your value proposition isn't compelling enough to make them switch from their current solution (or from doing nothing). The sales performance data alerts you to these potentially existential issues, prompting you to ask harder questions and, if necessary, have the courage to pivot your sales strategy, your targeting or even aspects of your core offering.

Finally, especially when you're just starting and the wins might be few and far between, use your metrics to set realistic goals and celebrate small victories. In the very early days, your goals might be more activity-based (e.g. 'I will send twenty personalised outreach emails this week' or 'I will book two first meetings') rather than purely revenue-based. As you begin to gather data on your conversion rates, you can set small, achievable improvement targets (e.g. 'This month, I want to increase my meeting-to-demo conversion rate from twenty percent to twenty-five percent'). Achieving these micro-goals provides a sense of progress and builds momentum, which is incredibly important for maintaining your motivation as a solo founder-salesperson. Every small improvement in your sales metrics is a step towards building a more predictable and scalable sales process for your growing venture.

KEY TAKEAWAYS

- Track inputs (activity), outputs (results) and outcomes (value) to fully understand your sales performance.

- The most powerful insights come from trends over time, not one-off results.

- Metrics without action are just numbers – use data to improve decisions.

FOUNDER'S FIELDWORK

Choose Five Core Metrics: track number of new leads, conversion rate, deal size, sales cycle length and churn rate.

Build a Simple Weekly Sales Tracker: use Google Sheets or Excel to log key activities and outcomes.

Conduct a Deal Retrospective: review your last three won and lost deals. What patterns or lessons emerge?

Calculate Your CAC and CLTV: use simple formulas to estimate Customer Acquisition Cost and Customer Lifetime Value.

Conversion Funnel Map: document your funnel from first contact to signed contract and identify biggest drop-off points.

Set a Monthly Review Rhythm: book a thirty-minute self-review to assess what's working, what's not and where to focus next.

Chapter twenty-four

STAYING AHEAD OF THE CURVE – ADAPTING TO MARKET TRENDS

'The only sustainable competitive advantage is an organisation's ability to learn faster than the competition.' – Peter Senge

Sales is not Static

The world of B2B sales, much like the entrepreneurial journey itself, is anything but static. It's a constantly shifting landscape influenced by technological advancements, evolving buyer behaviours, economic tremors and a host of other dynamic forces. What worked wonders to secure deals last year might feel a bit clunky next year and downright archaic in five.

Trendspotting as a Sales Advantage

For you, the startup founder who has bootstrapped your sales efforts from zero, thinking about 'market trends' might seem like a luxury you can't afford when you're just trying to land your next client. But here's the truth: staying ahead of, or at least in step with, these trends isn't a luxury; it's a crucial component of sustained success and, frankly, survival. This chapter is about how to keep your finger on the pulse without needing a dedicated research department and how to adapt your founder-led sales approach to remain effective and relevant.

Imagine you're navigating a flowing river in a small raft (your startup). Just paddling hard isn't enough if the currents are changing or new obstacles are appearing around the bend. You need to be looking ahead, anticipating the shifts and adjusting your course accordingly.

Failing to do so means you risk being swept into an eddy of irrelevance or, worse, capsized by a wave of change that you didn't see coming. For a startup, with its inherently limited resources and smaller margin for error, being caught off-guard by a significant market trend can be particularly perilous. Conversely, your agility as a founder means you can often adapt more quickly than larger, more cumbersome competitors, turning these trends into opportunities.

The good news is that you don't require a crystal ball or a massive budget to stay informed. It's more about cultivating a mindset of continuous learning and integrating a few simple practices into your routine. Your goal is to develop a 'weather eye' for the B2B sales climate, spotting the early signs of change and understanding their potential implications for how you find, engage and win customers. This isn't about chasing every fleeting fad but about making informed, strategic adjustments to your approach. So, where do you, the busy entrepreneur, look for these tell-tale signs of shifting market winds?

Your first and most valuable source is often right in front of you: your customers and prospects. The very people you engage with daily possess firsthand knowledge of the changes occurring in their industries and their buying processes. Revisit the principles of active listening from Chapter Seven. When you're having sales conversations or even informal check-ins with existing clients, listen not just for their immediate pain points but also for clues about how their expectations are evolving. Are they asking different types of questions? Are they mentioning new tools or processes they're adopting? Are they expressing new frustrations or aspirations? Their changing needs frequently serve as early indicators of broader market shifts.

Your competitors, even if you are in a very new niche, are another valuable source of insight. As discussed in Chapter Six (Market Research and Competitive Analysis), monitoring their activities isn't merely about understanding their current offerings. How are they adapting their sales and marketing messages? Are they embracing new technologies or highlighting different aspects of their value proposition? If you notice several competitors suddenly emphasising a particular feature or benefit, it might signal a response to growing market demand. You don't necessarily wish to replicate them but you should aim to comprehend the trends to which they might be responding. Subscribing to a few key industry publications, newsletters and blogs, relevant to both your industry and the B2B sales profession, can be a very low-cost way to remain informed. Many offer free content and often feature articles on emerging trends, new research and expert opinions.

Seek out sources that provide data-backed insights rather than merely speculative commentary. Similarly, engaging in relevant online communities and forums, particularly those where your ICP congregates (as discussed in Chapter Eighteen on Networking), allows you to see firsthand which topics are generating buzz and what new challenges your target audience is discussing.

Following key influencers and thought leaders in the B2B sales and marketing space on platforms like LinkedIn can also offer valuable early warnings or insights into emerging best practices. Look for individuals who consistently share well-researched, forward-looking content. Their perspectives can assist you in connecting disparate observations into a more coherent picture of what's changing. Be discerning of course; not every self-proclaimed guru possesses genuine insight but a few carefully selected voices can be very enlightening.

Technological shifts are a constant driver of change in sales. Maintain general awareness of new technologies that could impact how B2B sales are conducted. Artificial intelligence (AI) in sales, for instance, is moving beyond hype to offer practical tools for lead scoring, content personalisation and even the automation of certain types of outreach or follow-up. While there is no need to jump on every new tech bandwagon, understanding the potential of these tools to enhance your founder-led sales efforts' efficiency or effectiveness is crucial. Ask yourself, 'Could this new technology help me solve a problem, reach my ICP more effectively, or automate a time-consuming task without losing the personal touch?'

Economic shifts, whether global or industry-specific, invariably impact B2B buying behaviour. During periods of economic uncertainty or downturn, for example, buyers often become more risk-averse, prioritising solutions that offer clear ROI and cost savings, and that may involve more stakeholders in decision-making. Being cognisant of the prevailing economic climate helps you tailor your messaging and value proposition to resonate with their current priorities. If budgets are tight, emphasising efficiency gains or cost reduction in your UVP becomes even more critical.

Regulatory changes can also create significant market shifts, both for your business and for your clients. New data privacy laws, environmental regulations, or industry-specific compliance requirements can present new challenges for businesses, which in turn create opportunities for solutions that help them navigate these changes. Staying informed about significant regulatory shifts that affect your target market allows you to proactively adapt your offering or messaging to address these new pain points.

Let's get more specific. What kinds of trends should you be particularly watchful for in the modern B2B sales landscape? One of the most significant is the ongoing evolution of B2B buyer behaviour. Today's buyers are more informed and empowered than ever before. They often conduct extensive online research before engaging with a salesperson. They rely heavily on peer reviews, case studies and independent information sources. They expect personalised interactions and dislike generic, one-size-fits-all sales pitches. This means your sales approach needs to be less about 'telling' and more about 'guiding and advising', meeting them where they are, in their research journey, with valuable insights.

The desire for self-service is also growing. Many B2B buyers, particularly for simpler or lower-cost solutions, prefer to explore options, try out products and even make purchases with minimal direct sales interaction, if possible. This doesn't mean salespeople are obsolete; rather, it underscores the necessity for your online presence, your website and any self-service tools you offer, to be exceptionally clear, informative and user-friendly. For founders, this could involve ensuring your website clearly answers common questions or perhaps providing a straightforward, self-serve trial or a very basic free tier for your product, if it aligns with your model.

The sales technology (SalesTech) landscape is constantly evolving, presenting a bewildering array of tools. While it's easy to feel overwhelmed, the trend is towards tools that enhance efficiency, provide better insights and enable more personalised engagement, at scale. For a founder, the key is to seek accessible, affordable tools that address a specific problem for you. This could be a free or low-cost CRM that helps you stay organised (as discussed in Chapter Twenty-Three), a simple email automation tool for targeted follow-ups (but never a substitute for true personalisation), or tools that assist you in understanding who is visiting your website. The trend isn't solely about possessing the tools but about using them intelligently to augment your human efforts.

Communication channels continue to fragment and evolve. While email and LinkedIn remain B2B staples, the way people utilise them is changing. Video, for instance, has become increasingly significant – consider personalised video messages in outreach, video testimonials or short explainer videos.

Prospects may expect quicker responses on platforms like LinkedIn messaging compared to traditional email. Being aware of where your specific ICP spends their time, and how they prefer to communicate, is vital for effective engagement. Are they active in niche Slack communities? Do they respond well to interactive webinar formats?

The importance of data-driven sales is a trend that's here to stay. As we discussed in the previous chapter, even as a solo founder, tracking your basic sales metrics is crucial. The broader trend is towards using data not just to report on past performance but to predict future outcomes, identify at-risk accounts and personalise engagement based on a prospect's behaviour. While you may not have access to sophisticated predictive analytics tools initially, the principle of using the data you do have (e.g. email open rates, website engagement, conversion rates at different sales stages) to make smarter decisions is entirely achievable.

There's also a growing emphasis on value-based selling and clearly demonstrating ROI. B2B buyers are under increasing pressure to justify their expenditures. Simply listing features and benefits isn't sufficient. You need to articulate clearly and, where possible, quantify the specific business outcomes your solution will deliver for them. How will it help them increase revenue, reduce costs, improve efficiency or mitigate risk? The more tangible you can make this, the stronger your case. This often means digging deeper into understanding their specific business metrics and aligning your solution directly to those.

Finally, ethical selling, transparency and authenticity are no longer just nice-to-haves; they are increasingly demanded by B2B buyers. Prospects are wary of manipulative tactics, hidden fees or over-inflated promises. As a founder, your natural authenticity is a huge asset here. Being upfront, honest and genuinely focused on your customer's best interests – even if it means occasionally admitting that your solution isn't the right fit – builds immense trust and long-term credibility. This trend plays directly to the strengths of a founder-led sales approach.

Experimentation and Innovation in Practice

So, how do you, the entrepreneurial salesperson, actually adapt your approach in response to these trends without completely overhauling your strategy every six months? The key is agile iteration and a commitment to continuous learning. Firstly, maintain flexibility in your sales process. What worked for your first ten clients might need tweaking for the next fifty. Be open to adjusting your messaging, outreach channels, or even the stages in your sales cycle, based on what the market and your data are telling you. Don't become so attached to 'the way you do things' that you miss opportunities to do them better.

Continuously revisit and refine your value proposition (Chapter Three) in light of market trends. If a new technology emerges that changes how your ICP operates or if their primary pain points shift, due to economic pressures, your UVP might need to evolve to remain relevant. Your direct conversations with prospects are your best source of information for these adjustments. They will tell you, directly or indirectly, if your current messaging is resonating.

Commit to lifelong learning in sales. The skills and knowledge required to be effective in B2B sales are not static. Dedicate a small amount of time each week or month to your own professional development. This could involve listening to reputable sales podcasts, reading articles from trusted sources, attending free webinars on new sales techniques or even taking a short online course. Perhaps reading or listening to a book like this. Staying curious and open to new ideas is crucial.

Don't be afraid to experiment with new tools and tactics but do so in a lean, controlled manner. If you hear about a new outreach technique or a promising low-cost sales tool, don't bet the farm on it immediately. Run a small pilot. Try it with a small segment of your prospects. Track the results. Does it improve your efficiency or effectiveness? If yes, consider scaling it up. If not, learn from the experiment and try something else. Not every new trend will be a good fit for your startup or your sales style.

Perhaps most importantly, cultivate a mindset that is comfortable with change. The entrepreneurial journey is one of constant adaptation and sales is no different. Viewing change not as a threat but as an opportunity to learn, innovate and potentially gain an edge is a powerful psychological stance.

Your ability to pivot and adjust quickly is one of your greatest strengths as a founder. Build a simple 'learning loop' into your sales routine. This might involve:

1. Observe: actively look for trend indicators from your customers, competitors and industry sources.

2. Learn: understand the potential implications of these trends for your sales approach.

3. Hypothesise: formulate a small adjustment or experiment you could try in response.

4. Test: implement the adjustment with a segment of your prospects.

5. Measure: track the impact using your key sales metrics (Chapter Twenty-Three).

6. Adapt: based on the results, either roll out the change more broadly, tweak it further or discard it and try something else.

As a founder, you have inherent advantages when it comes to adapting to market trends. Your decision-making can be incredibly fast. You don't need to go through layers of bureaucracy to try a new messaging angle or test a new tool. You have a direct, unfiltered line to customer feedback, which is the richest source of trend information. Moreover, you have the ability to pivot your entire sales strategy relatively quickly if needed, something larger organisations struggle with. Use these advantages.

However, there are also pitfalls for the solo founder. One is the temptation to chase every shiny new object. With so many new tools, tactics and trends constantly emerging, it's easy to get distracted and spread your limited resources too thin, trying to do everything. Focus on trends that are most relevant to your ICP and your core business objectives.

Another pitfall is abandoning fundamental sales principles in pursuit of the latest fad. While tactics change, the core tenets of understanding customer needs, building trust and providing value remain timeless. Don't let the allure of a new trend overshadow these essentials. Finally, it's easy to become overwhelmed by the sheer pace of change. Accept that you can't master everything at once. Prioritise, take small steps and focus on continuous, incremental improvement.

While adapting to new trends is essential, it's equally important to remember that some aspects of successful B2B sales are remarkably constant. The need to deeply understand your customer's problems, the importance of clear and persuasive communication, the value of building genuine rapport and trust, and the necessity of delivering on your promises – these will always be critical, regardless of the latest technological advancements or shifts in buyer behaviour. Your ability to adapt to the changing 'how' of sales will be most effective when it's grounded in a solid understanding of the timeless 'why' behind successful B2B relationships. Staying ahead of the curve is about blending agility with these enduring principles.

KEY TAKEAWAYS

- Your market will change – adapt or risk becoming irrelevant.

- Reading the signals early gives you a competitive edge.

- Experimentation is not failure; it's evolution.

FOUNDER'S FIELDWORK

Track Three Industry Trends: subscribe to newsletters, follow thought leaders and check Reddit/LinkedIn groups for changes in your niche.

Ask Five Customers About the Future: 'What's changing in your industry right now that worries or excites you?' Log and analyse answers.

Experiment with a New Tool: test one new sales, comms or customer success tool this month – note what works or doesn't.

Conduct a Mini SWOT Analysis: list your startup's current Strengths, Weaknesses, Opportunities and Threats based on today's market.

Design a Quarterly Innovation Sprint: choose one process, pitch or offer to test and iterate every three months.

Chapter twenty-five

THE TRANSITION FROM FOUNDER-LED SALES TO HIRING THE FIRST SALESPERSON

'The job of the founder is to sell. The job of the founder is to stop selling.' – Anonymous startup wisdom

When (and Why) to Step Back

There comes a point in the life of a growing startup when the founder, who has bravely shouldered the entirety of the sales effort, looks up from their overflowing inbox and realises something profound: they can't do it all anymore. If you've reached this stage, take a moment to acknowledge what you've achieved. You've taken an idea, built it into a product or service and then personally convinced other businesses to pay for it. That's no small feat, especially if you started with zero sales experience. But as your business gains traction, your role inevitably needs to evolve. This chapter is about navigating one of the most critical transitions for any scaling startup: moving from founder-led sales to hiring your very first dedicated salesperson.

This isn't just a practical step; it's often an emotional one. Sales might have become your baby, just like the product itself. You know the nuances, the objections and the ideal customer intimately because you've lived it. The thought of handing over those crucial first conversations to someone else can be daunting. Will they understand it like you do? Will they represent your company with the same passion? These are valid concerns. However, this transition isn't about replacing you entirely; it's about amplifying your success and freeing you up to focus on other critical aspects of growing the business that only the founder can do. And here's the good news: because you've been in the sales trenches yourself, you're uniquely positioned to know what's needed and to guide that first hire effectively.

Recognising the right time to make this leap is crucial. Hire too soon and you might burn precious cash on a role that isn't yet sustainable or clearly defined. Hire too late and you become a bottleneck, stunting your company's growth because you simply can't keep up with demand while also trying to steer the ship, develop the product and manage everything else. Several signals will start flashing when the time is approaching. Perhaps you find yourself consistently dropping sales-related balls, leads aren't followed up on promptly, prospecting is sporadic or you're rushing through demos because you have product issues to fix or investor meetings to attend. If sales activities are constantly being pushed to the bottom of your to-do list due to other pressing founder duties, it's a strong sign.

Another key indicator is a reasonably consistent flow of leads. If your marketing efforts (however basic) or your own networking are starting to generate more inquiries than you can personally handle effectively, that's a good problem to have and one that a dedicated salesperson can help you capitalise on. It's also vital that you have at least a rudimentary, somewhat proven sales process in place. This doesn't mean a perfectly polished, multi-stage CRM workflow but you should have a repeatable method for taking a lead, qualifying them, explaining your value and closing a deal. You need something that can be taught, even if it's still evolving.

Of course, the financial reality is a major factor. Can your startup's revenue and cash flow realistically support the salary and any associated costs of a salesperson, even an entry-level one? You'll need to do the sums carefully.

Alongside this, solid market validation in the form of a growing base of paying customers provides evidence that there's a genuine, ongoing need for what you sell, justifying dedicated sales resources.

Finally, your own desire and need to focus on other strategic areas – perhaps scaling operations, developing new product lines or building out other teams – can be a powerful driver. If sales is preventing you from doing the high-level work that only a founder can do, it's time to find someone to take the sales baton.

What to Hand Over – and What to Retain

Once you've decided the time is right, the next step is to define what this first salesperson will actually do. It's easy to fall into the trap of expecting a 'sales superhero' – someone who will magically build a pipeline from scratch, create a sophisticated sales strategy and triple your revenue in their first quarter, all while needing minimal guidance. That's a recipe for disappointment. Your first sales hire, especially in a lean startup, is likely to be more focused on execution than grand strategy initially. Their primary role will be to take the sales process you, the founder, have developed (however informally) and run with it, systematise it and help refine it. Key responsibilities for an early sales hire will almost certainly include the prospecting for new leads (based on your ICP), qualifying those leads, conducting product demos or sales presentations, diligently following up and guiding prospects through to a close. They'll be on the front lines, handling objections and gathering market feedback.

They are not typically your VP of Sales or a Sales Manager; those roles come much later when you have a team to manage and a more complex sales operation. This first hire is about doing the day-to-day work of selling, freeing you up from those tactical tasks. Be very clear in your own mind what a typical day or week for this person will look like, based on your current successful sales activities.

Crafting the ideal profile for this pioneer is critical. For a startup, specific character traits and aptitudes often outweigh years of experience selling a similar product in a large corporation. You're looking for someone who is highly coachable, resilient in the face of rejection (which is inevitable in sales) and who possesses a genuine hunger to learn and grow with your company. They need to be comfortable with ambiguity and change, as your product, processes and market understanding will continue to evolve. An entrepreneurial mindset is a significant advantage – someone resourceful, proactive and unafraid to roll up their sleeves and figure things out with limited resources. While they don't need to be a carbon copy of you, they should be able to develop a genuine passion for your product and the problem it solves.

Strong communication and, crucially, listening skills are non-negotiable. They should be someone who can deeply understand customer needs, just as you've learned to do. You're also seeking someone who can potentially help systematise the intuitive actions you've been taking. Perhaps most importantly, in a small, early-stage team, cultural fit is paramount. This person will work closely with you and will have a significant impact on your company's early atmosphere.

Hiring, Onboarding and Enabling Your First Full-Time Salesperson

Finding this gem necessitates a thoughtful hiring process. Don't merely post a generic job ad and hope for the best. Tap into your existing network first. Referrals from trusted individuals are often the best source of quality candidates. LinkedIn is, of course, a key platform for sourcing and researching potential hires. Consider niche job boards relevant to your industry or to startup roles. Your job description should be both attractive and brutally honest. Highlight the exciting opportunity to make a real impact, to be a foundational member of the sales effort and to grow with the company. But also be transparent about the challenges and realities of working in an early-stage startup; it's not for everyone.

When it comes to interviewing, concentrate on assessing those key traits. Ask situational questions: 'Tell me about a time you faced a significant setback. How did you handle it?' or 'Describe a situation where you had to learn something new very quickly.' Role-playing can be incredibly revealing.

Provide them with a common objection you encounter and observe how they respond. Request that they conduct a mock qualification call or a brief product pitch after supplying them with some basic information. Evaluate their curiosity – do they pose insightful questions about your business, your customers and the role? As the founder, your active involvement in the interview process is essential. You're not merely assessing skills; you're evaluating fit and potential. And always, without exception, carry out thorough reference checks. Speak to their previous managers. Verify their claims and gain a genuine understanding of their past performance and work ethic.

Once you've identified your sales pioneer, setting them up for success through a comprehensive onboarding process becomes your next critical task. This isn't simply a half-day orientation where you hand them a laptop and a list of leads. For your first sales hire, onboarding is an intensive knowledge transfer from you, the founder, to them. They need to grasp your deep understanding of the product – not just its features but the core problems it resolves, its current limitations and the vision for its future. They need to internalise your ICP: who your ideal customers are, what their biggest pains are, what language they use and what motivates them to purchase.

You will need to meticulously guide them through your current sales process, step by step. What tools are you employing, even if it's just Gmail and a shared spreadsheet? What email templates or call scripts (if any) have you found effective? How do you usually handle demos or presentations? What are the common objections and how have you successfully overcome them? Allow them to shadow you on actual sales calls and meetings. There's no substitute for witnessing it done in real-time. Then, let them start doing it, perhaps with you listening in and providing immediate feedback.

Establish clear, achievable goals for their first thirty, sixty and ninety days. Initially, these goals should be more focused on activities and learning rather than purely on revenue targets. For example, 'In the first thirty days, conduct X number of outreach calls, shadow Y founder sales meetings and achieve proficiency in using our CRM.' Equip them with all the necessary tools – access to your CRM (even if it's basic), a professional email address, any sales collateral you've developed (however rudimentary) and a clear understanding of where to find information. Your role here is to be their primary resource and mentor.

As they ramp up, your role begins to shift from being the primary doer to being their manager and motivator. This is where the founder becomes the first sales manager. Regular check-ins and one-on-one meetings are crucial. These aren't for micromanagement but for providing supportive guidance, helping them troubleshoot challenges and offering continuous feedback and coaching. Listen to their experiences from the field – they are now your ears on the ground and will have invaluable insights.

Work with them to set realistic sales targets that evolve as they gain experience and as your lead flow becomes more predictable. Their compensation structure needs to be fair, simple to understand and aligned with early startup realities. This usually involves a base salary (to provide some security) combined with a commission or bonus structure that rewards performance. Some startups also consider offering equity to early pivotal hires like the first salesperson, to align their long-term incentives with the company's success. If you do, make these commensurate with performance and ensure that the equity is vested to reflect the impact of their activities over time. Remember to celebrate their small wins. Landing their first deal, or even just booking their first significant meeting, is a milestone worth acknowledging. Fostering a positive, supportive environment will be key to their motivation and retention. Your aim is to empower them to take ownership of their role while knowing you're there to provide a safety net and strategic guidance.

This transition also means an evolution in your own role as the founder. You need to learn to delegate real sales responsibility and trust your new hire to execute. This can be incredibly difficult, especially when you've been the one driving all sales success to date. Your focus shifts from doing all the selling yourself to enabling your salesperson to be successful. You become their chief problem-solver, removing roadblocks that prevent them from doing their job effectively. You might still be involved in particularly large or strategic deals where your presence as the founder adds significant weight or in situations where your deep technical knowledge is required. But your day-to-day involvement in every sales interaction will, and should, decrease.

Crucially, you need to actively solicit and value the feedback your new salesperson brings back from the field. They are now having dozens of conversations you're not privy to. What are they hearing about your product, your pricing, your competitors? This direct market intelligence is invaluable for refining your sales process, your messaging and even your product roadmap. The emotional journey for you, the founder, is about letting go of the operational details of selling while still staying strategically connected to the sales function.

There are several common pitfalls to avoid during this critical transition.

One is hiring too soon, before you have a reasonably validated product-market fit or at least a semi-proven, founder-led sales motion that can be taught. Another is hiring the wrong profile – for instance, a salesperson from a large, established company who relies on extensive resources, a well-known brand and a highly structured environment may struggle with the ambiguity and resource constraints of an early startup. Insufficient onboarding and a lack of ongoing support and coaching is another frequent mistake; you can't simply hire someone and expect them to figure it all out on their own. Setting unrealistic expectations for immediate, massive results can also demoralise a new hire and set them up for failure. Equally damaging is when the founder relinquishes all responsibility for sales, failing to provide the necessary support, guidance and strategic input. Moreover, not having even basic metrics in place to track their activity and performance against clear goals makes it impossible to manage them effectively or understand if they're succeeding.

When your first salesperson is consistently hitting their targets and the demand for your product or service starts to outstrip their ability to handle it all, that's a signal that you might be ready to think about hiring salesperson number two. The process you went through with your first hire, the defining of the role, the careful selection, the structured onboarding and the supportive management will provide an invaluable blueprint. Each successful sales hire builds on the last.

The transition from founder-led sales to building even a small sales function is a pivotal moment. It's a sign that your startup is maturing and has the potential to scale beyond your individual efforts. That first salesperson isn't just an extra pair of hands; they are a critical partner in your growth, a test case for your sales model and the foundation for your future sales organisation. Nurture them well.

KEY TAKEAWAYS

- Only hire once you have a repeatable, documented sales process.

- Your first full-time salesperson should scale what works, not invent from scratch.

- A great sales hire amplifies your approach, not replaces it wholesale.

FOUNDER'S FIELDWORK

Document Your Sales Process: create a step-by-step playbook or checklist for how you currently close deals.

Define Your Ideal First Hire Profile: list traits, experience and mindset of someone who can complement your sales style and market.

Prepare a Sales Onboarding Plan: outline what your first two weeks would look like for a new hire – tools, shadowing, scripts.

Create a Compensation Framework: draft a basic commission + base structure that aligns with startup constraints and incentives.

Decide What You'll Let Go Of: write down which sales activities you'll keep as founder and which you'll delegate – and why.

Hiring Criteria Matrix: list the top five qualities you need in your first salesperson (e.g. coachability, curiosity, sector experience)

FINAL WORD

A note from one founder to another

You've made it to the end – and that alone puts you ahead of most. Not merely because you've read a book on B2B sales but because you've chosen to embrace a facet of entrepreneurship that many tend to avoid.

Let's be honest: most founders don't dream of doing sales. It's rarely the exciting part. But it is the part that builds the business. The truth is, until you can sell what you've created, you don't have a company – you have a hobby.

This book wasn't written to transform you into a sales machine. It was crafted to assist you in selling in a manner that aligns with your values, your voice and your vision. It aims to demonstrate that selling can be structured, learnable and – believe it or not – even enjoyable.

So what now?

Now, you start, or restart, or continue, armed with the tools, the stories, the fieldwork and – hopefully – a bit more belief in your own ability to do this.

My invitation is this:

- Come back to this book as often as you need it.
- Share it with another founder who's struggling to sell.
- And stay connected – follow me or connect with me on LinkedIn https://www.linkedin.com/in/garrymansell/ mention that you have read the book.

Because selling isn't just a skill. It's a muscle. And the more you use it, the stronger and more natural it becomes.

I'll leave you with this:

Every conversation presents an opportunity to assist someone. Every sale demonstrates that your solution is valuable.

And every founder can learn to sell – particularly you.

Here's to your next conversation. Here's to your next customer.

— Garry

APPENDICES

APPENDIX A: IDEAL CUSTOMER PROFILE (ICP) TEMPLATE

Understanding exactly who you are selling to is the cornerstone of effective sales. Utilise this template to construct a detailed picture of your ideal customer. Revisit and refine it as you learn more from your sales interactions. (Ref Chapter 5)

ICP Name/Persona: (e.g. 'Growth-Focused Graham', 'Tech-Savvy Theresa')

1. Company Characteristics (Firmographics):
- **Industry/Niche:** (Be specific, e.g. 'Independent Craft Breweries', 'B2B SaaS for Project Management')
  - *Why this industry? Any specific regulations, trends, or challenges?*
- **Company Size:**
  - *Annual Revenue:* (e.g. £500k–£2m)
  - *Number of Employees:* (e.g. 10–50)
  - *Other relevant size indicators:* (e.g. number of clients, projects per year)
- **Location(s):** (e.g. UK-wide, specific regions, international if applicable)
- **Company Maturity/Stage:** (e.g. Startup, Scale-up, Established SME, Family-run)
- **Existing Technology Stack (if relevant to your solution):** (e.g. 'Uses Xero for accounting', 'Struggles with basic CRM')
- **Specific Company Challenges Your Solution Addresses:** (e.g. 'Inefficient lead follow-up', 'High customer churn', 'Manual reporting bottlenecks')

2. Key Individual Contact(s) within the Company (Personas):
- **Primary Job Titles you are targeting:** (e.g. Managing Director, Head of Operations, Marketing Manager)
- **Key Responsibilities:** (What are they accountable for?)
- **Their primary goals and motivations:** (What does success

look like for them in their role? What are they trying to achieve professionally?)

- **Their biggest challenges and frustrations related to your solution:** What keeps them up at night? What problems are they actively trying to solve?
- **How they assess success in their role:** (What metrics are they evaluated on?)
- **Their 'Watering Holes' (Where do they obtain information?):**
  - *Publications/Blogs:*
  - *Conferences/Events (Online/Offline):*
  - *LinkedIn Groups/Online Forums:*
  - *Influencers they follow:*
- **Their Typical Buying Process:** (How do they assess solutions? Who else participates in the decision? How long does it usually take?)
- **Their tolerance for risk and attitude towards new solutions and startups:** (Are they early adopters or more cautious?)
- **Common objections they might have include:** (e.g. 'Too expensive', 'Too new', 'Don't have time to implement')

3. Why They Would Choose YOU (Link to your UVP for this ICP):

- *Which specific aspect of your solution is most compelling for them?*
- *How does your approach uniquely address their problem more effectively than the alternatives?*

4. Negative ICP Markers (Who you are NOT targeting):

- *Company types which are a poor fit:* (e.g. 'Businesses <£100k ARR', 'Enterprise clients with >1000 employees', 'Companies in X unrelated industry')
- *Characteristics indicating a poor fit:* (e.g. 'No budget for new tools', 'Extremely resistant to change', 'Requires features we don't offer and have no plans for')

Date Created/Reviewed: Version:

APPENDIX B: UNIQUE VALUE PROPOSITION (UVP) DEVELOPMENT WORKSHEET

Your UVP is at the core of your sales message. This worksheet will assist you in clarifying what makes you unique and valuable to your Ideal Customer. (Ref Chapter 3)

Geoffrey Moore's UVP Template (Adapted):
- **FOR:** [Your Ideal Customer Profile – be specific, e.g. independent retail owners based in the UK]
- **WHO:** [Struggling with a specific problem or having an unmet need, such as being frustrated with managing stock across various online and offline channels]
- **OUR:** [Product/Service Name]
- **IS A:** [Category of solution, e.g. cloud-based inventory management platform]
- **THAT PROVIDES:** [Key quantifiable benefit or compelling reason to buy, e.g. a unified view of all stock in real time, reducing overselling by as much as 90% and saving 10 hours a week on manual reconciliations]
- **UNLIKE:** [The primary competitor or current alternative, such as reliance on spreadsheets and manual stock takes, or generic enterprise software that is overly complex and costly.]
- **WE:** [State your key unique differentiator – what sets you apart and makes you superior for this ICP? For example, provide a straightforward, affordable solution tailored specifically for the workflows of independent retailers, with direct founder support during the onboarding process.]

UVP Brainstorming – Key Questions:

1. Your Ideal Customer Profile (ICP) Reminder:

- Who are they, *really*? (Refer to Appendix A)
- What is their most *pressing and recognised* pain point related to your solution area?

2. The Problem You Solve:

- Describe the issue in *their* words. How does it feel for them?
- What are the *tangible negative consequences* of this issue? (e.g. lost revenue, wasted time, errors, missed opportunities, stress)

3. Your Solution (Product/Service):

- Name:
- Concise and clear description (1–2 sentences, no jargon):

4. Key Benefits & Outcomes (Translate Features into Customer Value):

Feature of Your Solution | *e.g. Automated Reporting*

Direct Benefit to Customer (What it *does* for them) | *e.g. Saves time on manual data entry*

Tangible Outcome for Customer (The *result* of the benefit – quantify if possible) | *e.g. Frees up 5 hours/week for strategic tasks; reduces reporting errors by X%*

Your Unique Differentiators (Why You?):

- What distinguishes your solution from direct competitors?
- What distinguishes it from indirect alternatives (e.g. status quo, workarounds)?
- What distinct advantages do you provide as a founder-led startup? (e.g. passion, niche expertise, agility, direct access, co-creation opportunities for early adopters)

5. Evidence/Proof (Even if early stage):
- Any initial user feedback? Results from beta testing? Personal experiences that led to the solution? Insights from industry knowledge?
- What steps can you take to make your claims more credible?

Drafting & Refining Your UVP Statement(s):
- **Attempt 1 (One-Sentence Version):** 'We help [ICP] who struggle with [Problem] to achieve [Outcome] by providing [Our Solution] which, unlike [Alternative], offers [Key Differentiator].'
- **Attempt 2 (More Narrative Version – a few sentences):**
- **Clarity Check:** Is it straightforward? Specific? Powerful? Free from jargon? Instantly comprehensible?
- **Compelling Check:** Does it address a genuine, pressing pain? Does it promise a worthwhile outcome? Does it make them eager to learn more?

Date Created/Reviewed: Version:

APPENDIX C: SALES CONVERSATION & OBJECTION HANDLING PLANNER

Effective sales conversations necessitate preparation, active listening and confident handling of objections. Use this planner prior to key interactions. (Ref Chapters 7, 8, & 11)

Prospect/Client Name:

Company:

Date of Conversation:

Objective for this conversation: (e.g. qualify need, book a demo, address pricing concerns, close the deal)

I. Pre-Conversation Preparation:

- **Key Information about Prospect/Company:** (Refer to ICP, recent news, LinkedIn profile, previous interaction notes)
- **Their Likely Pain Points/Needs (based on research/previous discussion):**
- **How Our Solution Specifically Addresses These:** (Link UVP)
- **Key Questions I Need to Ask (Discovery/Clarification):** (Open-ended questions)
    1.
    2.
    3.
- **Anticipated Objections & LAER Response Outline:**
  Anticipated Objection | e.g. 'It's too expensive.'
    - **L** (Listen – Key things to listen for) | Budget constraints, comparison points
    - **A** (Acknowledge – Empathetic phrase) | 'I understand budget is a key factor.'
    - **E** (Explore – Clarifying question to ask) | 'What were you comparing our price to?'
    - **R** (Respond – Key benefit/differentiator to highlight) | Reiterate specific ROI, value vs. cost. |
- **Desired Next Step/Call to Action (CTA):**

II. During the Conversation – Key Reminders:

- **Active Listening (70/30 Rule):** Let them speak 70% of the time.
- **Empathy & Rapport Building:** Show genuine interest.
- **Focus on THEIR Needs & Goals:** WIIFM (What's In It For Me?) for them.
- **Use Benefit-Led Language:** Translate features into outcomes.
- **Ask Clarifying Questions:** Don't assume; ensure understanding.
- **LAER Model for Objections:** Listen, Acknowledge, Explore, Respond.
- **Trial Closes:** (e.g. 'Does that sound like it could help?', 'How does that align with your priorities?')

III. Post-Conversation Actions & Learnings:

- Key Takeaways/Insights Gained:
- Actual Objections Raised & How They Were Handled:
- Agreed Next Steps & By Whom/When:
- What Went Well?
- What Could I Improve Next Time?
- Update CRM/Lead Tracker Immediately.

APPENDIX D: BASIC SALES PIPELINE TRACKER (SPREADSHEET EXAMPLE)

Even a simple spreadsheet can assist you in managing leads and monitoring your sales progress. Customise it to suit your specific sales stages. (Ref Chapters 13 & 23)

Columns:

Lead ID

Company name

Contact person

Contact email

Contact phone

LinkedIn profile

Lead source (e.g. Referral, LinkedIn, Website, Inbound Enquiry)

Date added

Last contact date

Next action date

Next action to take

Lead status (e.g. New contact, Qualified, Demo or samples scheduled, Proposal sent, Negotiation, Closed won/lost/on hold

Est. deal value

Actual closed value

Notes (e.g. Key pain points, interests, needs, objections)

ICP fit (High/Medium/Low)

Example Lead Status Definitions (Customise these for your process):

- **New:** Lead identified, no contact yet.
- **Contacted:** Initial outreach made (email, call, LinkedIn).
- **Engaged/Qualified:** Two-way communication established; initial qualification indicates potential fit.
- **Meeting/Demo Scheduled:** A discovery call or product demonstration is booked.
- **Proposal Sent:** A formal proposal or quote has been delivered.
- **Negotiation:** Terms are being discussed.
- **Closed – Won:** Deal secured, contract signed
- **Closed – Lost:** Deal did not proceed (note reason if possible).
- **On Hold/Nurture:** Not ready now but keep in touch for the future.

Simple Metrics to Calculate from this Tracker (Monthly/Quarterly):

- Number of New Leads Added
- Number of First Meetings/Demos Booked
- Number of Proposals Sent
- Number of Deals Closed – Won
- Total Value of Deals Closed – Won
- Conversion Rate: (Leads to Meetings, Meetings to Demos, Demos to Proposals, Proposals to Closed – Won)
- Average Sales Cycle Length (Time from Date Added to Closed – Won)

APPENDIX E: FIRST SALES HIRE – ROLE DEFINITION & ONBOARDING CHECKLIST

Transitioning from founder-led sales represents a significant step. This checklist assists you in defining the role and planning the onboarding for your first salesperson. (Ref Chapter 25)

I. Defining the Role – Your First Salesperson

- **Job Title:** (e.g. Business Development Representative, Account Executive, Sales Executive – choose based on primary focus)
- **Primary Objectives for the First 6–12 Months:** (e.g. Generate X qualified leads per month, Close Y new deals per quarter, Systematise current sales process)
- **Key Responsibilities:**
  - [ ] Prospecting & Lead Generation (Identify and qualify new leads based on ICP)
  - [ ] Conducting Outreach (Email, LinkedIn, Calls)
  - [ ] Delivering Product Demos/Sales Presentations/Product samples
  - [ ] Following Up with Prospects
  - [ ] Handling Objections
  - [ ] Guiding Prospects to Close
  - [ ] Maintaining CRM/Sales Tracker
  - [ ] Gathering Market & Competitor Feedback
  - [ ] Collaborating with Founder on Sales Strategy
  - [ ] Other:
- **Essential Skills & Experience:**
  - (e.g. 1–2 years B2B sales experience, OR proven track record in a customer-facing role with strong communication skills, experience in [Your Industry] is a plus)
- **Key Character Traits/Aptitudes (Crucial for Startup Fit):**
  - [ ] Coachable & Eager to Learn
  - [ ] Resilient & Handles Rejection Well
  - [ ] Proactive & Resourceful (Entrepreneurial Mindset)
  - [ ] Strong Listener & Communicator

- – [ ] Passionate about Solving [Our Customer's Problem]
- – [ ] Comfortable with Ambiguity & Change
- – [ ] Organised & Detail-Oriented
- – [ ] Team Player & Good Cultural Fit
- **Compensation Structure (Outline):**
  - – Base Salary Range:
  - – Commission/Bonus Structure Idea:
  - – Equity (If applicable):

II. Onboarding Checklist for First Sales Hire (First 30–60 Days)

- **Week 1: Immersion & Foundations**
  - – [ ] Welcome & Team Introductions
  - – [ ] Company Vision, Mission & Values (Founder-led session)
  - – [ ] Deep Dive into Product/Service:
  - – [ ] How it works, key features
  - – [ ] Problems it solves for customers
  - – [ ] Current limitations & product roadmap overview
  - – [ ] Understanding the Ideal Customer Profile (ICP) in detail
  - – [ ] Review of Current Sales Process & Tools (CRM, templates, etc.)
  - – [ ] Shadow Founder on live sales calls/demos (min. 2–3)
  - – [ ] Review existing sales collateral & messaging
  - – [ ] Set initial 30-day learning goals & activity targets

- **Weeks 2–4: Learning by Doing (with Support)**
  - – [ ] Start practising mock calls/demos with Founder
  - – [ ] Begin supervised outreach to a small batch of leads
  - – [ ] Co-deliver a sales demo with Founder
  - – [ ] Learn to handle common objections (role-play)
  - – [ ] Daily check-ins with Founder for questions & feedback
  - – [ ] Introduction to key internal processes (e.g. contract generation, invoicing if relevant)
  - – [ ] Start independent outreach, with call/email reviews by Founder
  - – [ ] Achieve proficiency in CRM/Sales tools

- **Weeks 5–8 (End of Month 2): Building Independence**
    - [ ] Conduct independent discovery calls & demos
    - [ ] Start managing own pipeline of leads
    - [ ] Participate in refining sales scripts/templates based on early experiences
    - [ ] Regular (weekly) one-on-one review meetings with Founder:
    - [ ] Discuss pipeline progress, challenges, learnings
    - [ ] Review key metrics (activity & early outcomes)
    - [ ] Achieve first small win (e.g. independently booked demo with qualified lead)
    - [ ] Set 60/90-day performance goals (more outcome-focused)

- **Ongoing Support from Founder:**
- [ ] Act as primary mentor & coach
- [ ] Be available for strategic deal support (e.g. joining calls for key prospects)
- [ ] Help remove roadblocks
- [ ] Continuously gather feedback from them about market/customer insights
- [ ] Foster a culture of learning and experimentation

APPENDIX F: NETWORKING & PARTNERSHIP OUTREACH TEMPLATE

Constructing your ecosystem is essential. Use these templates as a foundation for approaching potential networking contacts or strategic partners. Always personalise them (Ref Chapter 18)

1. Networking Follow-Up Email/LinkedIn Message (After Meeting at Event/Online)

Subject: Great to connect at [Event Name/Online Group]!

Hi [Contact's Name],

It was a pleasure to connect with you [yesterday/earlier today/last week] at the [Event Name/Online Group Name]. I particularly enjoyed our discussion about [Specific topic you discussed – be genuine!].

As I mentioned, I am the founder of [Your Startup Name], where we assist [Your ICP] in [Solving X problem/Achieving Y outcome].

[Optional: If you promised to send something, include it here: 'Here's that article/link I mentioned on [Relevant Subject]: [Link]']

I would be keen to stay in touch and learn more about your work at [Their Company Name]. Would you be open to connecting here on LinkedIn? Alternatively, perhaps we could schedule a brief virtual coffee sometime in the coming weeks if our paths happen to align?

Best regards,

[Your Name]

Founder, [Your Startup Name]

[Link to your Website/LinkedIn Profile]

2. Strategic Partnership Exploration Email/LinkedIn Message
Subject: Potential Collaboration between [Your Startup Name] and [Their Company Name]?

Hi [Potential Partner's Name],

My name is [Your Name] and I'm the founder of [Your Startup Name]. We specialise in [Briefly describe what your startup does and for whom, e.g. providing innovative data analytics solutions for e-commerce businesses].

I've been following [Their Company Name]'s work in [Their area of expertise/industry] with great interest, particularly [Mention something specific you admire or that shows you've done your research, e.g. your recent report on X, your approach to Y].

I believe there could be strong synergy between our companies. We serve a similar or complementary audience of [Your shared ICP] and I see a potential opportunity for us to [Specific partnership idea – e.g. refer clients who need Y service after they use our X product, co-host a webinar on the topic of Z, explore integrating our solutions to provide a more comprehensive offering].

Would you be open to a brief exploratory chat sometime next week to discuss whether there might be mutual value in working together?

Thank you for your time and consideration.

Best regards, [Your Name] Founder, [Your Startup Name] [Link to your Website/LinkedIn Profile]

Key Reminders for Outreach:
- **Personalise Thoroughly:** Generic messages get ignored.
- **Focus on THEIR Benefit:** Why should they care? What's in it for them?
- **Be Clear & Concise:** Respect their time.
- **Low-Friction Call to Action:** Make it easy for them to respond positively.
- **Proofread Carefully**

APPENDIX G: CONTENT IDEA GENERATION & REPURPOSING MATRIX

Consistently producing valuable content is essential for lead nurturing. Utilise this matrix to generate ideas and strategise how to maximise the impact of each piece. (Ref Chapter 16)

I. Content Idea Generation (Based on Your ICP's Pains & Questions):

ICP Pain Point/ Question	Potential Content Title/Angle	Content Format Idea (Blog, Video, Checklist, etc.)	Key Message/ Value for ICP	Call to Action (if any)
e.g. 'Struggling to manage remote team productivity.'	'5 Simple Strategies to Boost Remote Team Output This Quarter'	Blog Post + LinkedIn Summary	Actionable tips they can implement immediately.	'Learn more about our team collaboration tool?'
e.g. 'How do I choose the right CRM for a small business?'	'The First-Time Founder's Checklist for Selecting a CRM'	Downloadable PDF Checklist	Simplifies a complex decision, saves research time.	'Book a free consultation to discuss your CRM needs.'
e.g. 'Worried about new data privacy regulations in our industry.'	'Navigating [Specific Regulation]: What [ICP Industry] Needs to Know'	Short Explainer Video + LinkedIn Article	Clarifies complex info, reduces anxiety, positions you as knowledgeable.	'See how our solution helps with compliance.'

II. Content Repurposing Matrix:

Once you've created a 'pillar' piece of content (e.g. a detailed blog post, a webinar, a research report), consider how you can break it down and reuse its elements across various formats and channels.

Pillar Content Piece (e.g. 'The Ultimate Guide to X for Y ICP')	Repurposed Format 1 (e.g. LinkedIn Carousel of Key Stats)	Repurposed Format 2 (e.g. Series of 3 Short Email Tips)	Repurposed Format 3 (e.g. Script for a 2-min Explainer Video)	Repurposed Format 4 (e.g. Key Takeaways for a Tweet Thread)	Repurposed Format 5 (e.g. Checklist based on the guide)

Content Creation & Nurturing Reminders:

- **Focus on Value:** Educate, inform and solve problems. Avoid merely pitching.
- **Understand Your Audience:** Adapt content to their particular needs and level of awareness.
- **Be Consistent:** Consistent, valuable content fosters trust over time.
- **Simplicity is Effective:** You don't need a Hollywood budget for impactful content. Authenticity and relevance matter most.
- **Clear Call to Action:** Advise them on the next steps to take if they wish to learn more or engage further.
- **Promote Your Content:** Don't merely create it; share it across relevant channels where your ICP spends their time.

Continue Your Entrepreneurial Journey with More from

GARRY MANSELL

I genuinely hope 'B2B Sales for the Entrepreneur' has provided you with practical tools and the confidence to master a crucial aspect of building your business. The entrepreneurial journey is one of continuous learning and adaptation. If you've found this guide helpful, you may also benefit from my other books, each crafted to assist founders like you in navigating the exciting and often challenging realm of creating something remarkable.

Each book is rooted in real-world experience, delivering actionable insights to help you achieve your business ambitions with greater clarity and purpose.

Simplify to Succeed:
An Entrepreneur's Guide to Focusing on What Really Matters

In the whirlwind of startup life, complexity can be the enemy of progress. 'Simplify to Succeed' offers a practical framework for entrepreneurs looking to cut through the noise, streamline their operations and focus intensely on the core activities that drive genuine growth and impact. Discover how to declutter your thinking, prioritise effectively and build a more focused, productive and ultimately more successful (and less stressful!) business. If you're feeling overwhelmed by the sheer volume of tasks on your plate, this book will help you identify where your true leverage lies.

'A breath of fresh air! Garry's approach to simplification has genuinely changed how I run my business.' Amazon.co.uk Reviewer

'Packed with actionable advice that you can implement immediately. Highly recommended for any founder feeling swamped.' Verified Purchaser, Amazon.co.uk

Find 'Simplify to Succeed' on Amazon.co.uk and other good bookstores.

50 Golden Rules:
The Beginner's Guide to Entrepreneurship

Are you embarking on your entrepreneurial journey? This book serves as your essential roadmap. '50 Golden Rules' distils decades of experience into concise, actionable advice covering everything from cultivating the right mindset and crafting a successful strategy to effective execution and authentic leadership. Each rule provides a timeless principle to guide you through the challenging yet immensely rewarding path of starting and growing your own business. Think of it as your pocket mentor, offering clarity and encouragement every step of the way.

'Wish I'd had this when I first started out! So many invaluable nuggets of wisdom in one place.' Amazon.co.uk Customer

'Garry has a knack for making complex ideas simple and actionable. These rules are genuinely golden.' Entrepreneur, Amazon.co.uk Review

Search '50 Golden Rules: The Beginner's Guide to Entrepreneurship' on Amazon.co.uk and leading book retailers.

Thank you once again for investing your time with me through these pages. I wish you every success in your sales efforts and your broader entrepreneurial journey. Stay connected, keep learning and never underestimate your ability to create something remarkable.

Garry Mansell